The Silver Lining

The author in 1945

The Silver Lining

Memoirs of a Fighter Pilot

by

Ray Gerard Smith, DFC

To Eric

Ray Smith F/Lt D.F.C.

The Memoir Club

First published in 2006 by
The Memoir Club
Stanhope Old Hall
Stanhope
Weardale
County Durham

British Library Cataloguing in
Publication Data.
A catalogue record for this book
is available from the
British Library

ISBN: 1-84104-162-9

Typeset by TW Typesetting, Plymouth, Devon
Printed by CPI Antony Rowe, Eastbourne

Contents

List of Illustrations

Preface

The origin of the book goes back a few years, to a time when the chairman of a local group (known as the Friends of St James) of which I was a member invited me to be 'speaker' at one of their monthly meetings and give a talk on my experiences in the RAF. I said that I would be pleased to do so. So far so good. But how was I to make a decent presentation out of dozens of stories already in my mind? The one thing that I did not want to do was to deliver a rambling speech without any form to it. We had had one or two like that and no matter how interesting the subject matter it was a pain to listen to them.

Obviously, the times of greatest danger, when I nearly lost my life, had to be included. Listing these showed four occasions during my Spitfire days, four on Typhoons and one later which terminated my career. That made nine and so I had my title *Nine Lives* on which to build a story. Other remembered incidents could be used to frame the critical ones, such as, for instance, how I came to be sent to Malta in 1942, where three of the four danger spots on Spitfires occurred. For the Typhoon section, the change from air-fighting to ground attack could be emphasised with other incidents from that time.

I wrote out my talk in full and then read it slowly to myself against the clock. It came, I think, to about forty minutes, which, allowing for referring to my headline notes here and there, would give about forty-five minutes in all. The chairman agreed to this length of time, provided, of course, that the audience were sufficiently interested. I thought that there would be no doubt about that. As time for the talk approached I became nervous. I had not done any speaking for many years and while I had not forgotten the basic 'tricks of the trade', I was well and truly out of practice. On the night itself I could have wished myself to be elsewhere, but once I was on my feet the nerves eased off and, apart from having to refer to my notes a time or two, everything went smoothly and the audience seemed to appreciate it. Questions and answers followed about how anybody accepted such risks. I replied that although I had done my fair share, I had no idea how young men, some barely over school age, could go out day after day or night after night to face the appalling risks that went with the job, and I still don't have the answer.

My wife and daughter were in the audience and they both said afterwards that they knew nothing of what I had been talking about. A subsequent talk

I gave about the many silly and amusing things that happened in the RAF apart from flying was probably not quite as interesting, but brought forth the same reaction from my wife and daughter. This set the ball rolling. My wife said that it would be a pity if all these memories were to die with me, leaving a vacuum for the grandchildren and generations to follow. So I started to write it all down, the difficulty being that one memory triggered another so that the text was continuously being altered to fit in the latest memories that came to mind. I think that this process is now complete and if anything of consequence comes to mind in future it will have to be shunted aside for the present.

Memory, of course, is subjective and I am well aware that others will have different recollections of the same events. However, this is my story based on my memories.

Acknowledgements

To my wife Lorna, whose idea it was to commit my memories to print.

To my daughter Laraine, who edited my first version and put it on tape.

To my son Professor Paul Smith, who worked on innumerable alterations and produced three versions of the manuscript.

To Lionel Swain, who typed the major part of my first attempt at writing the story.

Chapter 1

Enlisting

After leaving school in summer 1939 I was looking for a suitable position in which to start work. There was no financial urgency but shortly after the declaration of war (how I remember the near panic when air-raid sirens sounded about ten minutes after Neville Chamberlain made the facts known on radio) I got a job as a laboratory assistant. It involved two long walks and a half-hour train ride to get there and so early rising was of the essence. After about nine months in the job the 'phoney' war came to an abrupt end when Germany invaded Holland, Belgium and France. Belgium and Holland were soon overrun by the German army, which then, with the *Luftwaffe*, tore France apart and the Dunkerque evacuation took place. I felt very strongly that I must do my 'bit' for the war effort and took the decision to join the RAF, having always been interested in aircraft. My parents were not too keen but made no effort to stop me.

It proved to be rather more difficult actually to enlist in the RAF than I had expected. At the first recruiting office I went to I completed a form with details of name, address and occupation, which I listed as 'laboratory assistant'. The sergeant said, 'No trade in the RAF for laboratory assistant – next!' I attempted to explain that I wanted aircrew but he took no notice. He was one of the pig-ignorant NCOs who seem to flourish in the services and should not have been let anywhere near a recruiting office. My next attempt at another office produced a similar result. Finally I went to an office in Acton where the sergeant was younger and intelligent. Listening to what I wanted to do, he asked me what I would do if I couldn't get aircrew in the RAF, to which I answered that I would go for the army's tank corps (like hell I would!). He seemed to like my answer and asked me to wait with some other men. A couple more joined us in the next hour, then the sergeant came over and said that aircrew training was being greatly expanded but they couldn't take any more for the time being. We could either go home and wait to be called or we could join straight away and get some service time, pending our time to be sent for flying training. We all said we would like to join straight away, although it meant losing the privileged lives we had been leading.

A few days later I received orders to report to Cardington, Beds. The group of us who had met at the office the previous week arrived on the little train which puffed from Bedford to the platform at Cardington. Another half-dozen we did not know came as well. Amongst them were some pretty tough looking individuals who obviously had not had an easy life, but this caused no problems. We rattled the gate and a sergeant came out and said, 'What do you b——s want?' We answered that we had come to join the RAF, and making the remark 'God help us', he opened the gate and phoned for another sergeant to come and see us. This he did, first showing us the bell tent, which was to be our home while we were there. This had twelve straw-filled palliasses and pillows, each with two blankets. He said, 'Dump your things here,' then took us to the airmen's mess, where we were fed with cold fried fish and slabs of bread, followed by pineapple chunks. I was starved and it went down a treat. We were then conducted back to our tent and our privileged life was already a fading memory.

The tent was obviously designed for the Crimean war, when men averaged 5′6″. Our feet all stuck out beyond the pole. We all had to lie on our side and draw our knees up and stay that way. One man brought out an automatic pistol, which he started to clean, but he was roughly disarmed by others and the gun thrown into a ditch. Once our sergeant was out of sight, the tougher ones went out in the evening light, found a way out of the camp and spent their last evening of freedom roistering in Bedford before coming back the same way. I was amazed that anyone would take the risk of being caught, but these men had no respect for authority.

We managed to sleep fairly well and in the morning three of us went to the airmen's mess again and had a whopping breakfast. When we got back to the tent the sergeant was there and bawled out, 'Where the 'ell have you been?'

I said 'We have had our breakfast.'

He swelled up, turned red and said, 'You wha?' Let me tell you you'll have your f——in' breakfast when I say you'll have your f——in' breakfast and not at any other f——in' time – UNDERSTAND?' The last word was delivered at ninety decibels from a range of twelve inches and was accompanied by a generous spray of best sergeant's spittle down the front of my jacket.

The rest of the time at Cardington is a bit of a blur. I must have taken an oath but I do not remember it. I do remember long lines of naked men shuffling past weary doctors. One of the doctors checking my chest expansion said, 'I wish I had your lungs, son', and so do I now. Onto the dentists' room where twelve dentists offered only one treatment, which was extraction. As most of the men could never have attended a dentist, business was brisk. Fortunately my parents had paid to have my teeth cared for and when my turn came, the dentist just looked in and said, 'You're all right.' We were given a vaccination in one arm and an inoculation in the other so we could sleep only on our backs that night. We were issued with uniforms then marched to the tailors' shop where mysterious chalk marks were put on. As there were only three or four men on sewing machines doing alterations, I believe that, except in the case of a bad misfit, the chalk marks were rubbed off and the uniform returned unaltered. Finally, we were given brown paper and string to wrap up our civilian clothes and address home. Our last contact with civilisation was severed and I became 1169270 AC2 SMITH, R.G.

Chapter 2

Start of Ground Training

The next morning we were given two one-inch thick cheese sandwiches and an apple and were put on a train for Blackpool, where we did a fortnight's square bashing on the promenade, with many other squads doing the same. We were a motley bunch, from ex-slum-dwellers to public schoolboys. The squad of about two dozen men and the drill sergeant were one's life. Other squads we never met. Drill sergeants were not the sort of people one would take home to tea, but they had a genius for turning a civilian rabble into smart, disciplined and proud service men in fourteen days flat and then had to start with a fresh lot. Rather wearisome, I would have thought.

If we were marching somewhere, as distinct from doing drill, we were obliged to sing, and failure to strike up a tune brought threats from the sergeant. 'Sing, you bastards or I'll have yer' was a favourite phrase. During the time doing square-bashing in Blackpool, our squad was marched to the baths and we all changed into swimming trunks (many borrowed from the baths' staff) and our squad sergeant said, 'Hands up those who can swim.' A few of us, including me, put our hands up so the sergeant said, 'Show us how it is done, Smith.' He did not know that I was an expert but I dived in and did a couple of lengths of free-style. As I came out, the sergeant looked away and said nothing. We went to the baths quite often after this, sometimes as a squad, sometimes as individuals. It made a lovely change from 'Right! left! right!' and 'Keep in line, damn you,' although we were getting much better at the drill stuff. A few days later we had an athletics meeting at which the sergeant said, 'Let's see who can run a mile.' As a trained athlete I set off and just about lapped the field. Again the sergeant said nothing. Senior NCOs could not abide squad members who were expert at something. This one eventually got his own back when the squad was doing something at which I was hopeless, probably cricket or boxing, when he said 'Blimey, we have found something that Smith can't do.'

With others I was billeted in civilian B&B premises and was fed quite royally. Extra inoculations were given which entitled one to twenty-four hours excused duty. One of the boys in our digs fainted clean away and his head flopped into his dinner, but no harm done. A few days before we left, two squads were lined up face to face in a building. We had our trousers and underpants round our ankles and our shirts and vests pulled up while two NCOs walked side by side between the lines with torches to examine our genitals for signs of the clap or crabs. Somewhere up the line one NCO said, 'Blimey, what have you been doing with that, son? Fall out and report sick.' This caused a lot of laughter, soon silenced by the NCOs. We tried to figure out how this was done to women coming into the services, but concluded it was not done at all. I made the acquaintance of a nice-looking girl after working hours one day and arranged to meet her at the fun park the next day. My idea was to get her on the 'Big Dipper' rail cars to frighten her into screaming and holding on to me. She must have read my mind because she didn't turn up; surprise, surprise.

At the end of the course there was a 'marching' competition under the eagle eye of the officer commanding. The squads vied with each other to be the smartest and snappiest at the prescribed drill. My squad did not win it, much to the chagrin of our sergeant who apparently had fancied our chances. After a passing-out parade (passing out was indeed happening, with many men fainting in the heat) which lasted three hours, we spent our last night in Blackpool. Next day we were given two one-inch thick cheese sandwiches and an apple (this seemed to be standard travelling rations) and were put on the train to Yorkshire, landing up at Leconfield, which was a fighter station.

We drilled and stuck our bayonets into dummies and were eventually given rifles but, of course, no bullets until we went on the firing range. I was not very good because I couldn't stop myself from blinking while firing, but it was a good day out. While we were all banging away at the targets with our ancient rifles, the noise was considerable. A young recruit just down the line from me burst into tears. The sergeant took his rifle from him and said, 'Take him back to his mummy, he's no f——ing good to me.' He did not belong to our hut and I don't know what happened to him.

I really had a love affair with my beautiful rifle. I never envisaged killing anyone with it but it was a beautiful thing. It was a Short Lee-Enfield, very easy to handle and comparatively light. Some of the men got Ross P80 rifles from the First World War. These were probably more accurate, having a peep sight instead of the V-sight of the Enfield, but were a lot heavier. Rifles were cleaned with a '2 by 4'. This cloth came in a roll four inches wide and torn off in two-inch strips. It was soft and absorbent but I cannot remember whether it was pushed through the barrel or pulled through. After cleaning, an NCO would come and peer down the barrel to check if it had been done properly. He would then give the gun back and the owner would snap the bolt forward and click it down to the lock position.

In our hut there were twelve Englishmen and twelve Scotsmen. Whether this was by accident or design I do not know, but at least neither had the advantage over the other. One day when I was off duty, I was lying on my bed when a Scotsman who had been washing some clothing came in. His bed was almost opposite mine and he flung his wet socks over the sill of the open window and turned away to drop his other wet clothes over his bed. When I looked a minute later his socks, apparently of their own volition, were sliding over the sill towards the outside. I shouted, 'Watch your socks' but by the time he tried to grab them they had vanished and all he saw was the back of an airman scuttling off with his prize.

The one thing that no one ever did was to go into another hut and neither did anyone invite someone from another hut into their own. A hut was closed society and set its own rules for twenty-four men to live together. Not that peace was assured by any means, but arguments were settled within one's own group. There was some teasing and taunting remarks between the Scots and the English and I tried not to react at any aimed at me, because I was terrified of fisticuffs. One day, however, I came into the hut and found a Scotsman stretched out on my bed. I asked him to move but he just sneered at me. So I surprised myself by up-ending the bed and sending him crashing to the floor. Then I jumped over the bed and landed heavily on him. We wrestled around and when his arm came up he smashed his precious wrist watch on the bed, whereupon he got up and left me alone. No one else had a go at me after that.

We were drinking beer at the NAAFI one evening and I put down my empty glass upside down. An old soldier sitting nearby picked up my glass and put it the right way up and said 'Do you know what it means, son, to put your glass like that?' I said I didn't and so he told me that it meant that I would fight anyone in the room. Did I want to do that? I never did that again, but I was surprised by the tolerance of old soldiers towards overgrown kids like me.

On another day when we were off duty we saw a hangar being draped with the Polish national colours with all of the several hundred Poles lined up inside. A short while after, a light plane landed and General Sikorski got out and went into the hangar to address his men. Afterwards they sang their national anthem. It was very moving.

One of the tedious events was the fortnightly pay parade. I must have attended one previously but have no memory of it. When there were two or three hundred men it took a long time, particularly, of course, for those whose initials were well down the alphabet. When one's name was called one snapped to attention, called out the last three figures of one's service number and then advanced to the table where a clerk and an officer sat. After saluting, we received the money, then saluted again and marched away. We were entitled to twenty-eight shillings but for some reason we only received just £1. The missing eight shillings was the amount a married airman had sent home direct to his wife. Married men were very much in the minority so the RAF gave itself the job of keeping records of umpteen thousands of single men in order to give them their back-pay later on. I believe we got our back-pay when we became sergeant pilots. Very welcome it was, but in the meantime my mother helped out with a ten-shilling note in the post at intervals until we started flying. The rate of two shillings per day would buy a couple of pints of NAAFI beer and a packet of Woodbine cigarettes. It would take about £7 per day to get the equivalent today. The main problem was that if one had the notion of taking a girl out it meant no beer for the previous week. Failure to make a suitable female acquaintance then meant that the money saved was promptly spent in the pub. According to the older hands on the station, the tea was laced with bromide to stop us feeling too sexy. Enough to stop the testosterone-fuelled randiness of very young men would have meant them being too dopey to do any work. The story was obviously to tease us.

During our stay, our blankets became infested with some bugs and if anyone had told me earlier that I would sleep soundly while sharing my bed with nasty insect life I would not have believed them. Our blankets were sent to Driffield (a bomber station a few miles away) for delousing and they came back a few days later full of broken glass and had to be individually shaken. This arose because the Germans had got wind of the fact that the idiot commander at Driffield had his ageing Whitley bombers lined up wing-tip to wing-tip as if on parade (or so we were told) and the Germans sent over some bombers from Norway to deal with this, acting presumably on the idea that all our fighter squadrons were fighting in the South. Actually there was a British fighter squadron at Leconfield along with a Polish one just completing their training (they were all experienced pilots). The two squadrons soon caught up with the German bombers and very few, if any, got back to Norway. But Driffield had already been smashed up – hence the glass in the blankets.

The only other event of any consequence was a riot we had in our hut. We slept on telescopic beds, which were easy to sabotage by slipping the bottom of the bed past the catches designed to keep it in one piece. If one went out to the toilet after dark one's bed might be interfered with, so that when one settled down somebody would pull a string so the bed collapsed in the middle. Putting it back together in total darkness and remaking it was a nightmare. We slept on three small mattresses put together and these were called 'biscuits'. On a shelf over the bed were a folded towel, shaving gear and a tin mug with knife, fork and spoon, commonly known as 'mug and irons'. What caused the riot, I think, was that someone at the far end of the hut found his bed had been tampered with. In a fury he flung his three biscuits down the hut in the dark. These hit others who promptly retaliated by hitting others and in a matter of minutes we had a full scale riot with biscuits flying everywhere, with a loud clatter when someone's shelf was swept clear. The noise was deafening and somebody must have gone to our sergeant to tell him about it. He came at a gallop but an officer got there first, put the lights on and bawled 'Attention!' We froze and the officer said to our sergeant who came running up, 'If you can't control your men I'll get someone who can.'

That did it. The sergeant let us get to bed after cleaning up. A little while later he came back, threw the door open and said, 'Beds made and fully dressed in five minutes.' In pitch darkness the panic was beyond belief and when he came back we were not half ready. He looked around and said, 'I'll teach you bastards to get me into trouble.' He did this again, so we decided to stay dressed with our beds in daytime make-up, ready for him to do it a third time. Of course, he knew what we would do and no doubt went happily to bed leaving us sitting in the dark. It was about 1 a.m. before we finally dared to go to bed. There were no more riots.

Postings for aircrew finally came through and for the first time in my life I saw naked envy from all those not going and heard some nasty remarks and threats of violence. Fortunately, the senior one amongst us was a very tough hombre whom nobody had dared to tackle and he said to us, 'Don't react. We'll be out of here tomorrow.' So we left the next day with, guess what? Two one-inch thick cheese sandwiches and an apple!

Chapter 3

Initial Aircrew Training

Our final destination after leaving Leconfield was Babbacombe in Devonshire, but after leaving King's Cross our little party split up, some to go home for an hour or two; in my case, my parents were at the station. I expect we spent an hour or so together but I cannot really remember. Crossing London to Paddington I caught the Torquay train, eventually arriving at the guardhouse in Babbacombe about 1 a.m. I was instructed to sleep on the floor, which I find almost impossible because I have so little padding on my bony frame.

The next day I joined several dozen aircrew wannabees in a hotel on the front where we were given white flashes to put in our caps. We were told that from now on we had to wear our webbing belts suitably whitened and were not allowed to speak to members of the public. I do not know the reason, but it put paid to our usual spare time occupation of 'cherchez la femme' and was thus pretty unpopular. Even if one's parents came to visit one could speak to them only in their hotel and not in the street. We were permitted to swim from Babbacombe beach (then shut to the public) and were told that the rather tired-looking diving platform was 'out of bounds'. The services never learned of the futility of making places out of bounds when they were easily accessible to people who could not subsequently be identified. We swam out to the platform and turned it over, after which it sank. Typical vandalism of youth and our CO made a stink, but nobody owned up.

We were frequently disturbed by air-raid warnings at night and we all had to troop in darkness to a brick-built shelter at the back. It was absolutely packed but one of our party smuggled a girl in and while he was enjoying himself the CO shone a torch in and spoiled his fun. The girl hastily got her clothes straight and fled, trampling on us as she went out. The CO then gave us a talk by torchlight on morals and letting the side down and other such rubbish. On another night we were making quite a noise in the shelter when our corporal shouted, 'Shut up, you lot, or I'll come in and sort you out.' A very public school voice in the darkness said 'If you come in here, corporal, you won't get out again.' This put him in a terrible rage but after a bit of shouting he went away.

As far as I can work it out this must have been in the middle of August 1940. We spent several days at Babbacombe, being split in squads of about

D Flight No. 1 Squadron. 3 ITW Torquay

a dozen men in each and then marched to No. 3 ITW (Initial Training Wing) in Torquay, each squad being billeted in one of the commandeered hotels. Our hotel was on the corner of Victoria Parade and Beacon Hill and we slept in what had been the dining room. A very large hotel in Victoria Parade was the mess hall for all the squads. There were lurid stories circulating about badly burned German bodies being washed ashore. I do not think that any of these were true but I do believe that lengths of pipe were put down in shallow water through which petrol could be pumped which could be ignited when it floated to the surface in an attempt to fry Germans attempting to come ashore. There was, however, no confirmation or denial of this of which I was aware. In the event of an invasion we were to be marched inland but to what end I do not know.

In authority over us was an officer (who had been a golf pro) but he had several squads to look after so we didn't see much of him. We had our very own flight sergeant who was a right bastard and a corporal who was nice enough. Shortly after we settled in, the flight sergeant came round after breakfast to view how we had put the room in 'daytime' order. He walked round making comments about our lousy bed tidying and when he got round to me he kicked my bed over (it was no worse than any of the others) and said, 'Right, Smith, let's start again, shall we?' He then harried me for ten minutes or so while I tried to make it perfect. Eventually he said that was how he wanted every bed put up for the day. He picked on me because I was by far the youngest and most naive one there; such is the way of the bully. He probably had at the back of his mind that I was very unlikely to retaliate by beating him up one dark night. There were others amongst us who certainly would have done.

We had lessons and we marched and marched and had lessons. I have long since forgotten what most of the lessons were about and can only suppose that we were given some information about airframes and engines, the theory of flight, basic aerodynamics, elementary navigation, etc. We did learn the Morse code and something called airmanship, whatever that was. The classrooms were scattered about Torquay and we marched from one to the other and I think often two or more squads attended the same lessons. The marching was accompanied with loud singing. On one day we were left in charge of the corporal who marched us to Cockington Forge, about four miles, I think. There was a nice pub there, where the corporal bought himself a pint of rough cider while we all had half a pint, which cost 3d and was very strong. The corporal seemed to be enjoying himself so we each put a penny in the kitty and bought him another pint. He was soon seeing the world through rose-tinted glasses but the third pint was a mistake and he became deeply unconscious. It occurred to us to wonder what we were going to do with an unconscious corporal miles from home.

Fortunately a bus came along and we filed on carrying the corporal and, by sitting either side of him with an elbow across his chest, we kept him upright. No one charged bus fares to servicemen in those days and in a few minutes we were back in Torquay. I cannot remember for the life of me what we did with the corporal; probably half carried and half dragged him to our billet and put him to bed. For us, being back so early, we had a heavenly two hours of nothing to do and no one to chase us around.

I think the course took eight weeks or so and there were exams to be taken at the end of it. Not too intellectually demanding but I did quite a bit of swotting to make sure of the result. Unfortunately I got a paralysing sinus headache, the first that I had ever had. I had to go to the sick bay for some painkillers. These were called APC tablets and were strong enough to allow me to pass the exams. But afterwards I felt awful and had a day in bed which I got away with because the sergeant was elsewhere.

We went on a long leave of fourteen days. I believe I dallied a bit in London, where I saw some pilots with shockingly burned faces and sometimes hands as well. A number of society girls undertook to accompany them to shows and restaurants and to look them right in the face no matter what disfigurement the pilots had suffered. To my mind it was a very brave thing to do and probably saved the sanity of many of the men. No doubt many of the girls cried themselves to sleep at night. When I got home I mentioned this and my mother said, 'They really shouldn't let them out.' I had no answer to this appalling remark but must have wondered what the situation would have been if I had turned up without a face.

Orders came through for me to report to No. 7 Elementary Flying Training School (EFTS for short) at Desford in Leicestershire and flying in Tiger Moths began in November 1940.

Chapter 4

Initial Flying Training

Upon becoming a trainee pilot, my rank became LAC (Leading Aircraftsman) and my pay rose from 2/- for a day to a fabulous 7/6 (37½p but about £19 in present money). This at first seemed wealth indeed but one soon learns how to spend it. Funnily enough, this is far more money than I ever spend now.

Being mid-winter we had to wear full flying clothing (a warm quilted inner with wind-proof outer) with two pairs of gloves and a helmet with goggles, and even then it was cold. The aircraft used for initial flying training was the famous Tiger Moth (of which some examples still exist) This aircraft was very safe, provided one did not behave like an idiot. To start with we flew dual with an instructor and mine was PO Males. He took me on a brief flight for air experience and to become familiar with the cockpit. I had to be able to touch and use all the controls and instruments without looking. This was on 22 November and on the same day he took me for a longer flight, showing the effect of controls, taxiing and level flight.

The next day there were two further flights to which climbing, gliding and stalling were added and on the second flight medium turns to left and right. On 24 November there were two more flights with 'taking off into the wind' being added. On 25 November there was only one flight with gliding approach and landing. I learned to take off, turn round the airfield (always anti-clockwise) and then land again. Colloquially this was known as 'circuits and bumps'. A few of our course simply could not judge distances and failed, being sent off to be air-gunners or observers. Engines were started by swinging the propeller by hand. This had to be done in a certain manner to avoid the propeller taking one's arm off when the engine fired. When not flying we often had to swing propellers for those who were, so we learned the trick of the preservation of our extremities. As far as I can remember, flying was interspersed with lectures and studies, probably alternating morning and afternoon, and of course dependent on the weather.

On 26 November there were two more dual sorties including powered approach, landing and spinning. At first I found the latter disconcerting, to say the least, with the horizon not where it should be and spinning round me. Once I got used to it, it ceased to be alarming, and recovery from the spin was easy enough.

After a flight with PO Males on 28 November, the chief flying instructor gave me a test on all that I had learnt so far, then he got out and sent me off solo after just seven hours and ten minutes of dual flying. Nervous before, of course; exultant afterwards, again of course. But beyond that I had a feeling I can only describe as 'empowerment' to do what most people never have the chance of doing, and doing it well. After this, bouts of dual instruction followed with solo ventures as well. Side slipping was introduced and also low flying (great fun), instrument flying (with a hood over the cockpit), more spinning, climbing turns, steep turns and forced landing. I was introduced to aerobatics on 17 December and greatly enjoyed it, except on one occasion when there had been a party the night before. My instructor, I think, knew about it and he flung the aircraft about until I very nearly pleaded for mercy, but at least I was not sick. Eventually there were cross-country flights where the instructor sat in the back and I flew from point to point map reading. I cannot recall learning to use the CSC (course and speed calculator) in initial training. This was for navigating and map reading was a supplement to this.

Later on in the eight-week course, a dozen of our Tiger Moths went off to fly to Yorkshire. There were six instructors and six trainees flying. Six of the aircraft were left in Yorkshire and the other six flew back with two in each one. My instructor got lost on the way home and we force-landed in a field with a wavy surface (something to do with the way ancient Celts cultivated their fields, I believe) and after much bouncing around we came to a halt. We were immediately surrounded by farm folk and the farmer himself took us to his house and we were fed with a huge fry-up, after which we were escorted to the pub and beer was poured into us. After staggering back we were put two in a bed, which the instructor liked as little as I did. During the time at the farm and in the pub I wore my inner flying suit zipped about half way up. I cannot explain my reason for doing so unless I did not have any trousers on, which seems unlikely.

Before all this had taken place the instructor had phoned the CO at Desford to tell him where we were, and the next morning a car turned up with a senior instructor to decide whether the plane could be flown out or would have to be taken to pieces. He decided he could do it. So after watching his rather hair-raising take-off we returned to the airfield in the car.

While at Desford I developed an unrequited passion for the landlady's daughter at the pub by the level crossing, but soon got fed up with the unrequited bit and, when a comely land-army girl in a car stopped and asked if I wanted a lift, I accepted with alacrity and she was my date for the rest of my stay there. Sometimes she would let me know that she would be bringing another girl with her next time so I would invite my friend

The author (right) with his instructor after a forced landing in 1941

Gordon Springthorpe to come along. We enjoyed ourselves, usually going to a hotel where steak and chips could be had for 1/6, which is 7½p. A few drinks and a good snog completed the evening. When there were just the two of us, the young lady liked to talk about the farm where she worked and was at pains to describe to me the technicalities of mating bulls and cows. Whether this was to get me and perhaps herself aroused I have no idea. I was much too naive (not to say innocent) to make a move. So if that is what she wanted her efforts were wasted.

Two of the pupils were older than the rest of us and I believe one had been a policeman. The other had been in the merchant navy before the war. He had a pink baby face with slightly bucked teeth and looked as if he wouldn't say boo to a goose. Nothing could have been further from the truth and when a bully threatened him he got the surprise of his life, receiving a severe beating for his trouble. The pupil said that he had deliberately been beaten by the bosun on his first trip to teach him what might happen if he spoke out of turn.

While we were at Desford, the heavy bombing of Coventry took place. This was close enough for us to see the glow in the sky caused by burning buildings. It must have been hell on the ground and it was the misfortune of the population to have acres of industrial buildings in their midst.

The pupils had their own mess and so did not have to sit with the other airmen for meals. It meant less rush and noise and we could have a drink or play cards without going to the NAAFI. I remember being asked to make up a foursome at bridge. I said that my knowledge of the game was rudimentary, but the three said, 'Never mind, we don't play seriously.' So I joined in and within a few minutes was being accused of bad calling, bad leading and every sin in the bridge player's book. I got up, threw my cards on the table, made some tart remarks and left them to find another victim.

Towards the end of the course I came across PO Males in a pub in Leicester. He had had a few, put his arm around my shoulder and told his friends that I was his star pupil. I think the drink had more to do with this comment than my ability, but I was thrilled to hear him say that.

If there were any exams for ground work I do not remember them and on completion of the course, with sixty-two flying hours, I was posted with others to No. 15 Service Flying Training School (SFTS) at Kidlington near Oxford in January 1941.

Chapter 5

Service Flying Training

My instructor at Kidlington was Flight Sergeant Gilbert, a quiet and patient man devoid of the shouting so beloved by many senior NCOs. I was very lucky to be one of his pupils. On our first trip he took me up in a Harvard aircraft which was used to train fighter pilots. I was overjoyed by this but that was the only flight I had in that aircraft. A change of policy made Kidlington over entirely to twin-engined Airspeed Oxfords, an aircraft I never did get to like for some reason. It also meant that I was being trained to be a bomber pilot which I did not want at all.

My first flight in an Oxford was of course 'air experience' and cockpit layout and lasted only fifteen minutes. A second flight the same day covered the effect of controls, taxiing, straight and level flight and medium turns. This for forty minutes. The next day another forty minutes added flying on one engine, stalling, climbing and gliding with powered approach and landing. The next day there were two flights totalling sixty minutes which included taking off into the wind and gliding approach and landing. After another two trips I was sent on my first solo flight. While not having the

The Airspeed Oxford. Photo courtesy of MAP Sleaford

impact of my first solo on Tiger Moths, it nonetheless gave me great satisfaction. It had been just four hours and forty minutes to get there.

The course continued, expanding into forced and precautionary landings, instrument flying, map reading and navigation, with continuing practice of taking off and landing, slow flying, low flying, single engine landings, steep turns, side slipping and finally night flying. Much of this was conducted from Weston-on-the-Green, an airfield a few miles away. The aircraft would fly there after the first exercise of the day and fly back on the last exercise of the afternoon. For night flying we stayed at Weston. The flare path was made of real paraffin flares, which had to be lit by hand. If the enemy came at all close, nearby airmen had to run along and put out the flares until the all-clear was given. I remember only one occasion when this happened.

Taking off at night was easy enough until I had left the flare-path behind and found myself in complete darkness with nothing visible on which I could orientate, and so it was straight onto instruments. Except in hazy weather, there was usually a clear horizon and so one did not have to concentrate all the time on the instruments. The Oxford had the full night-flying panel including the artificial horizon and digital course indicator, by means of which the pilot can keep himself right way up, can make turns, climb and dive and any other manoeuvre that is necessary. The direction indicator was set against the compass reading before take off. Turning could be done on the compass reading itself, but this meant having to overshoot the compass turning one way and undershoot turning the other, so direction indicator was easier to use.

Rather to my surprise I found flying at night quite easy and very enjoyable. There was no connection with the ground other than by radio and when flying solo I found the solitude and detachment from the world outside very comforting. I was my own master for a while. I believe the approach to landing was assisted by an 'angle of approach' indicator situated on the ground. This showed beams of light and I had to keep the colour green by adjusting the flight path. If I went too low it showed red and too high showed yellow. This was a great help and made the approach landing easy. What did fox me was trying to fly by an instrument called the 'kicker'. The idea was to fly down one radio beam giving the letter 'A' in Morse code in the centre. The kicker instrument showed a needle responding to the dot-dash. If you ran off to one side, the Morse for the letter 'N' (dash-dot) started, but it did not tell you which side of the beam you were on. In addition, the dots and the dashes showed with the regularity of a metronome and I found the greatest difficulty in deciding whether I was listening to dash-dot or dot-dash. I do not remember mastering this exercise. Not the least attraction of night flying was being served up with thick bacon sandwiches with lots of rashers in them, together with hot cocoa without milk but lots of sugar. This came round about midnight and was very welcome.

Without instructors we flew in pairs of trainees or solo as instructed. When flying in pairs one trainee was designated as pilot and occupied the left-hand seat. On one occasion when flying as a pair my room-mate and I decided to return to Desford and without permission landed there to see if we could say hello to anyone we met while stationed there. There wasn't anyone we knew so we took off and flew back to Kidlington where of course we were late and instructors were beginning to panic. We were wheeled in front of the flight commander who gave us the edge of his tongue. Actually I think the instructors did not mind their trainees being a little adventurous but they had to go through the motions of disapproval.

During the course we suffered our first fatality. A particular friend of mine crashed in the field before reaching the airfield and was killed. I felt very badly about this and never found out how it had happened. At the time it seemed so unfair that someone could be killed who had never raised a finger to anyone. I became an atheist and this lack of religious belief stayed with me for many years.

The course ended early in May 1941 by which time I had a total of nearly 150 hours of flying. I got my wings and became a sergeant pilot. There was a total lack of ceremony. The stores NCO called out 'two sets of stripes and two pairs of wings' for each pilot, just throwing them down on the counter. The contrast with the American large-scale ceremony with brass bands and senior officers was really quite funny.

After we had hurriedly stitched on our sergeants' stripes and wings, we went into a lecture room where the CFI gave us a talk thus. 'Now you have your wings you all think you know all about flying. Take it from me you are only just beginning and my hope for your sake is that you have an accident at about 500 hours of flying, not a bad one to hurt yourself but to give you a good fright and make you think. At about 1,000 hours I hope you have another one then you might begin to be a good sensible pilot!' My timing was a bit out but accident-wise I followed his hopes exactly.

While at Kidlington we often went to Oxford in a group, drinking and chasing girls. On one occasion I saw a girl I liked and said, 'Haven't I seen you before somewhere?' Of all the corny approaches! A short while after I saw her again and asked her to come with me to the cinema. To my shame I took out the publican's daughter from Kidlington the night before and she stung me for a steak and chips, which left me stony broke, and so when I met the other girl at the cinema she had to pay. Our relationship grew and later on when I was on operational flying and went back to Oxford to see this young lady I can remember dancing (very badly) in Oxford Town Hall with this lovely sexy girl in my arms, the whole of this very ordinary experience being given a vivid intensity by the ever-present thought in the back of my mind that I might not live to do it again. That lady has now been my wife for over sixty years. She says that my being broke and expecting her to pay is a habit to this day. Fortunately, this is a joke between us and not taken too seriously.

Again I presume there was course work at SFB and again I have no memory of it. Obviously I must have done well enough or I would not have got my wings. Much to my surprise I was posted to a fighter Operations Training Unit (OTU for short) whereas all the rest went to bombers, as far as I could find out. This I think was partly due to my habit of flying the staid Oxford like a fighter and partly to my instructors' realisation that I was too wayward and undisciplined to make a steady bomber pilot. I also like to think that Flight Sergeant Gilbert thought that my natural talent for flying would be wasted trundling around in a large bomber.

CHAPTER 6

Operational Flying Training

BEFORE MOVING ON to fighter training at OTU, a few notes about fighter aircraft of the day. They all shared common features such as main wheels (retractable of course) under the wings and a small wheel under the tail. This caused the aircraft to be very nose-up in attitude on the ground, with the result that the pilot could not see anything in front of his aircraft. Taxiing meant swinging from side to side using the brakes and following a zigzag path. On take-off, as soon as the tail came up, full forward vision came back.

The other common feature was the potentially lethal one of the fuel tank being positioned immediately in front of the pilot, except in the case of the Messerschmitt 109, where the pilot sat on it. The tank had a self-sealing outer skin but this was not effective against multiple bullet strikes which almost always caused a massive fire. If the pilot was uninjured and the aircraft still controllable, he had less than ten seconds to go through the routine of getting out of the aircraft without being badly burned. The terrible burns suffered by some pilots were due to their not being able to get out quickly enough. Those still alive who could not get out at all were burned to death, unless mercifully they hit the ground first.

At the end of May 1941 I turned up at No. 52 OTU at Debden in Essex all alone, but was soon put into the system. The aircraft there were Hurricanes. They were rather old aircraft but still had 50 per cent more power than the two engines in the Oxford put together, while being much smaller. Hurricanes were single seaters and no dual instruction was possible. I did, however, have a few hours of dual and solo on Miles Master aircraft, which were training aircraft for fighters. I had to learn the Hurricane cockpit so we could touch and operate all the knobs and levers blindfold.

I was a little nervous before my first flight in a Hurricane, but this gave way to the tremendous thrill of opening up 1,000 h.p. of Merlin engine to give what seemed to be a rocket-like take-off. Then followed a session of circuits and bumps, during which one of our number came in much too fast and instead of opening up and going round again he floated down the runway before landing. The result was that he ran off the end of the runway at speed, through the hedge and perimeter wire, over the road and through another hedge and into a field where he came to his senses and pulled his wheels up before he ran into anything else. He was not popular with the flight commander, one Flight Lieutenant Frank Carey DFC, but I don't think that he was punished.

A problem that I encountered for the first time was that the gyro instruments 'toppled' when banking over 90°. This resulted in the artificial horizon flopping about uselessly and the direction indicator spinning around out of control. The DI could be caged to prevent this but the AH could not. This was to avoid a pilot, who had been doing aerobatics or been in a dog fight and who broke away into cloud, thinking that he was flying straight and level because the AH was central, whereas he may well have been diving or stalling and well on his way to killing himself. In American aircraft, the AH could be caged and accidents happened.

Numerous airborne exercises followed: high level and low level flying, flying in formation, navigation and cross-country pin-pointing of targets, dummy attacks and dusk landings. It was all very enjoyable and I began to feel like a real fighter pilot, especially in the 'attack' exercises and dogfights or 'air combats' to use the official term. When flying at dusk, we were guided home by a neon flashing beacon which could be seen twenty miles away. Before taking off we were briefed about which letter of the alphabet the beacon would be flashing in Morse code. We were also told the bearing one had to fly from the beacon, which was several miles away from the airfield, to find our flight-path. The electric flare-path itself consisted of a row of hooded dim blue lights down each side of the runway. It could not be seen at all from a few thousand feet up. These lights did not illuminate anything on the ground.

Off duty I did have a girl friend but am ashamed to say that I remember nothing of her or about her at all. A lot of our spare time was spent skinny dipping in a small lake a mile or so away and sunbathing afterwards. If any females came along we made no effort to cover ourselves and so they fled. I cannot imagine a modern miss fleeing from such an encounter, but things were very different sixty years ago.

There was a story about our flight commander Frank Carey, who, for some reason, had fallen out with the local farmer. To get his revenge, Frank used his .22 rifle (with which he was a dead shot) and he started to shoot some of the flock of prize pigeons which lived at the farm. We used to see him sneaking off with his rifle. News of this reached the Station Commander's ears, which was unfortunate for Frank since it was the SC who owned the pigeons and the farmer was only providing board and lodging for them. Frank was promptly sent to the Far East where he became an ace against the Japanese.

Also at OTU we had a number of Czech pilots, one of whom was a Count, no less. They were rather a wayward lot. One of them had an engine failure and he crashlanded in a field well away from the runway.

A Flight No. 52 operational training course, Debden – instructors and pupils

The ambulance roared off and while they soon found the aircraft the pilot was missing. Hearing sounds of feminine laughter, the crew went up to the back garden of a large house and saw the pilot at his ease amongst a bevy of beauties. To him this was much more important than reporting to the station that he had crashed.

At Debden there were things called armadillos, one on each side of the runway. Basically these were heavy lorry chassis covered all over with sheet steel with a couple of machine guns sticking out of the top. We asked what they were for and were told that in the winter of 1940–41 when the *Luftwaffe* bombers were all over England, the flare-path was lit for the fighters who were hoping to see a bomber. During one night an unidentified aircraft landed. From the control tower it was made out to be much bigger than a fighter, and after landing the aircraft followed the taxi-track round and stopped below the control tower. The pilot left his engines running, came up the stairs and into the control room, where he went up to the duty officer sitting at his dimly lit desk and said 'Wo bin ich, bitte?' The officer, not thinking, said, 'Actually, it's Debden, old boy', before realising that the question had been asked in German. He looked up and the pilot realising that he had answered in English looked down. They stared at each other for a few seconds before the pilot spun on his heels and ran for all he was worth back to his aircraft where he shimmied up the little ladder and slammed the hatch. He then taxied round the rest of the taxi track and took off again. Nobody was armed at the time. The station commander evidently thought he would become a laughing-stock and, in spite of the astronomical odds of it ever happening again, he got the armadillos from somewhere and these were always manned when the flare-path was lit.

A friend of mine at Debden had a little red Ford car (new price just £100 then). He took me around Saffron Walden and occasionally to Bishop's Stortford or Cambridge. He used some aircraft fuel, which was stained a bright orange colour and, by wiping the stain off the carburettor, he got away with it. On one occasion, after a disagreement with some of the foreign pilots, they retaliated by pushing his car into the field at the back of the sergeants' mess and then jacking it up first at one end and then the other. They removed the wheels, which they stacked up, and then lowered the car back onto its axles. It presented quite a problem lifting the car up high enough to get the jack under it again.

I think it was at Debden that I first made the acquaintance of an infernal machine called the 'Link Trainer', the purpose of which was to give instrument flying exercises without leaving the ground. It was like a primitive simulator but I did not get on with it at all. The controls were so floppy and totally without 'feel' and I never did learn to do well on it.

So much for OTU at Debden. I now had nearly 200 hours of flying, and in the middle of July 1941 1 was posted to No. 74 (Tiger) Squadron, then at Acklington in Northumberland. After some leave at home, my friend in his little car called for me to take me to Acklington to which he was posted. I remember my mother asked him to take care of me, which, although he was older than me, caused me some embarrassment. We drove up the A1, which was then little better than a country road, stopping for the night in York before going on to to Acklington in Northumberland.

CHAPTER 7

Operational Flying

BEFORE GETTING ON to the subject of my experience in flying against the enemy, I would like to write a little about how aircrew adapted to the risks and, in many cases, the appalling strains involved. As I see it there was a minority that possessed complete self-command (as against mere self-control). They were able to armour themselves against fear and dread and most survivors of this group wound up much decorated and in high positions. Below them were some aircrew who had the sublime conviction that nothing was ever going to happen to them, while at the other extreme there were those of a fatalistic nature who knew they were going to be killed so gave up worrying about it. Then there were those who were too thick and unimaginative to worry about anything – in some instances, not a bad way to be.

I did not fit into any of the above. I and thousands like me simply used up our nervous reserves, with wide variations between people as to how long they could keep going. One particular event just before D-Day drained more out of me that I would have thought possible, as will be made clear later in this story. The RAF gave all aircrew 'operational rest' periods when they became instructors for a few months. Even the best needed to recuperate from their exertions to sharpen up again, and a rest greatly extended the operational usefulness of those like myself who had perforce to live on their nerves.

We reported in at 74 Squadron, which had received a battering the year before in the Battle of Britain and I didn't think there were many left amongst the pilots who had been through it. Some NCO pilots, however, were obviously strained and it showed. We seldom met the officers, but probably the remaining old hands were in no better shape than the NCO pilots.

The aircraft were Spitfire Mk. II and, after learning the cockpit drill, the flight commander said I was to fly around for a while and not to go far away. As it was, I did not go far enough away, because the Spitfire was a revelation of just how good an aircraft can be. Its instant reaction to the slightest touch on the controls by the pilot made the pilot and the aircraft into one entity and I was so at home in it that I started doing loops and rolls and other aerobatics, all of which the flight commander saw from the ground. When I landed, flushed with delight, he gave me a dreadful

A line of Spitfire Mk. II. Photo courtesy of MAP Sleaford

dressing down for not obeying orders to fly round a bit and then land. The truth was that with my pride in my flying skills and at only nineteen years of age, I was too cocky by half to please my superiors, and more experienced pilots of my own rank probably thought I was a pain in the neck.

The squadron practised formation flying and dummy attacks on other aircraft and patrolled the north-east coast. Pairs of us were scrambled now and then to chase Germans we never saw. On one occasion my leader had to return to base because his aircraft was malfunctioning and I was left on my own looking for a German aircraft in between the clouds. I was terrified to the extent that I left my throttle at full power and maximum revs so the engine started to overheat and I did not know what to do. Happily I was recalled before doing any damage.

A main memory of my short time with 74 Squadron is about the man in charge of the ground crew. He was, of course, a flight sergeant and so was always addressed as 'Chief'. He had sailed the world before the war in the Fleet Air Arm and probably visited every den of iniquity in every port. His knowledge of English grammar was rudimentary but for all that he could express himself very forcefully. On one quiet summer afternoon all was peaceful and Chief was in his little office. Suddenly the scramble bell rang and the clerk bellowed out 'Squadron scramble'. When the Chief erupted out of his office he yelled to his men, 'Get down them kites a bit f——in' swift.' It was only a practice to make sure that we were all awake but the Chief's expression has remained with me ever since.

Acklington airfield in Northumbria was close to a small mining village where the slag heap had been burning inside for years, with some smoke and steam escaping to the atmosphere. One evening just as shifts were changing, the slag-heap blew up, badly burning many men. Some of them were treated at the camp hospital.

On the airfield itself, a lot of night flying was going on, while frantic efforts were being made to develop airborne radar. The pilots, of course, had to try and sleep during the day, but were being woken up by announcements over the public address system. One day the door of one of the huts occupied by the nightfliers burst open and a Canadian came out in his pyjamas with a revolver in his hand and yelled, 'I can't sleep for that f——ing thing' and put bullets into the two nearest loudspeakers. He may have got some sleep that day but was no doubt punished for his action.

This flying was done in Boulton Paul Defiant aircraft which had a gun turret just behind the pilot. The gunner could bring to bear a heavy fire to the rear and an automatic cut-out prevented him from shooting his own tail off. Some of these aircraft were used in the latter part of the Battle of Britain and gave some *Luftwaffe* fighter pilots attacking them a very nasty surprise. But the German pilots soon got round this by attacking head-on. The losses of the Defiants led to their being withdrawn from daylight service. They were painted black and used as night fighters.

I think it was at Acklington that I first saw the new Beaufighter with twin radial engines and a formidable armament of forward firing guns of 4x20 mm cannon and eight wing-mounted machine guns. Once the correct radar was fully developed it was installed in the Beaufighter and the observer in the rear seat guided his pilot onto an enemy aircraft until the pilot could see the enemy's exhaust. At this point he could close in and shoot it down. This did much to discourage night bombing raids by the enemy.

During my stay with 74 Squadron, an invasion exercise was carried out. There was still concern that, while a full invasion plan had been scuppered by our fighters defeating the *Luftwaffe*, there was still a possibility of heavy raids by the *Wehrmacht* against airfields near the coast. Aircrew were confined to barracks while the exercise lasted. Presumably we were too valuable for us to get injured. I have no idea whether the exercise was declared satisfactory, but one thing that I was sure of was that the 'enemy', being army troops from around the locality, did not penetrate the area where our chief was in charge. He armed his men with screw pickets, which are a heavy spiral of steel about three feet long with a wicked point at one end and a knob at the other. These men set about them, much to the harm and detriment of the unfortunate soldiers.

At intervals a lorry was provided to take the pilots who wished to go out after hours to visit the local town. The furthest we went was Newcastle, on a couple of occasions, when we went to the Assembly Rooms where dancing was in progress. I met a comely WAAF girl. We did not stay at the dance and walked down to the Tyne bridge behind the girders without being seen. Very nice too.

We also visited Morpeth about which I remember nothing. A visit to the mining town of Ashington was more notable. I met a girl who had a magnificent figure but she declined to let me fondle her. It did not matter much because fighting broke out on the dance floor between RAF men and locals. Instead of running away, as I would have expected, the girls, including my date for the evening, stood on chairs and cheered on the fighters to greater efforts. I did not want to get involved and was saved from doing so by the arrival of the RAF police who rapidly grabbed the fighting airmen and dragged them out.

In early September 1941 I was posted to 616 Squadron at Westhampnett (satellite of Tangmere). The squadrons there had been Douglas Bader's wing but he had been shot down a couple of weeks previously. 616 Squadron had some famous pilots among their number, including 'Jonnie' Johnson, 'Cocky' Dundas, 'Nip' Hepple and a New Zealander, Flight Sergeant West, amongst others whose names I cannot recall. Flight Lieutenant 'Cocky' Dundas was flying in his last operation of his tour but had to return with something the matter with his aircraft. He was absolutely furious and I was surprised that anyone was angry because he couldn't get at the enemy. I had thought that one would have to fight but not that anyone actually wanted to do so.

Upon arrival I was ordered to drop my kit in the sergeant pilots' quarters, which were two huts side by side with a door in between. Somebody said, 'That's your bed', indicating the one by the communicating door. I did not realise at the time that this was the 'new boy's' bed but I soon found out. When we went out drinking in Chichester there was one pilot in the other hut who, instead of being content with just drinking a lot like the rest of us, got stoned out of his mind and had to be part-carried/part-dragged back and plonked on to his bed. The trouble was that when he woke up in the small hours bursting to relieve himself he was disorientated by the beer and the total blackout and did not always find the outside door. I was sleeping by the inside one and woke up to find myself in a warm version of Niagara Falls. I got up with a yell to wake the dead and felt my way across to the other side of the hut where I would be safe. There was much laughter at my expense, but I'm glad that he was obliged to clear up his own mess the next morning.

The aircraft were Spitfires Mark V, more powerful than the Mark II, but still armed with eight machine guns. We flew fighter sweeps up and down the channel and into northern France. Some of these sweeps drew no response from the Germans. With my inexperience I always flew as No. 2 to an experienced pilot and my job was to stick with him like glue. The first time that we ran into a dogfight I felt terror and amazement, in equal measure, at this seething mass of aircraft, to the extent that I lost sight of my No. 1. Having no idea how to extricate myself in safety, I went into a defensive turn (no German fighter can stay in a turn with a Spitfire). After going round two or three times, I realised I wasn't seeing any other aircraft in the sky. Both sides had gone home and I was left circling like an idiot in mid-channel. When engaged in another dogfight I at least managed to stay with my leader.

On 616 Squadron I saw the 'finger-four' formation being used operationally. The habit in the RAF of flying in threes had cost many lives. The Germans had realised that the basic fighting formation was a pair of aircraft, one of the pair being the leader. A group 'flying in threes' being attacked or attacking meant that a pair was not possible and it was some time before the RAF realised the trouble it was giving itself by flying in 'Air Display' formation.

There were only six operational sorties that I flew from Westhampnett, little enough, but it was an apprenticeship for what was to come later. At some time during my time there, I was obliged to act as one of the pall bearers for the funeral of one of our NCO pilots who had been shot down. I remember the coffin was very heavy which may have been sealed as there were no deep freeze mortuaries. In my atheistic frame of mind, the funeral service seemed very cruel to me. Later on I realised that a funeral at least gave a dignified closure to the life of a colleague or loved one. This is better by far than having him vanish as though he had never been, which was the case for the bulk of the RAF fatalities. I hope that the mourners of that occasion did not realise that what was in the coffin was an unrecognisable mass of flesh and bone dug up from the crash site.

I have one other memory of Westhampnett. I arrived late in dispersal one morning. This was unforgivable as other people had been up since dawn and expected to be relieved on time. The Flight Commander put someone else in my place and then ordered me to run round the perimeter track carrying my parachute. Running wearing soft flying boots was difficult enough, but running carrying a heavy parachute with dinghy pack, about thirty pounds in all, was agony. The pack bumped heavily upon one's bottom with every step and it was too heavy to carry in one's arms. On top of this one had to endure the jeers and catcalls from other squadrons' dispersal and the perimeter track was about one and a half miles right round. I was never late again!!

In the middle of October 1941 the squadron moved to Kirton-in-Lindsey in Lincolnshire. The nearest town was Scunthorpe, which was a 'steel' town and was a dreadful dump of a place. While on a trip there by RAF lorry, I decided to go for a haircut. The salon was full to bursting and the only chair available to sit on was a hairdressing chair at the end of a row of them. I sat down expecting to wait at least an hour when one of the hairdressers came along, plugged in his clippers and cut a furrow up the back of my head. He then said, 'It's not your turn', pulled out the plug and went to start someone whose turn it really was. This left me with a furrow in my hair so I had no option but to wait until it was my turn which seemed a very long wait.

Already in residence at Kirton was an 'Eagle' squadron comprising a wild group of experienced American pilots who had volunteered their services to the RAF. They also flew Spitfires and were commanded by an upper-crust Englishman with accent to match and a double-barrelled name. The Yanks greatly revered him and he had no trouble controlling them.

On one occasion I flew to Potters Bar and put on an exhibition of aerobatics over my parents' home. My mother apparently fainted with fright at seeing her only son throwing an aircraft around. Under Squadron Leader Colin Gray we practised interceptions and patrolled the Lancashire and Yorkshire coasts. The squadron leader himself made a brilliant display of airmanship in one practice when he dived down behind us and then pulled up, rolled on his back and came in perfect position to shoot down our leader. He then pulled the stick back and looped away to our rear. Later on he made a name for himself as a wing commander in North Africa. 'Jonnie' Johnson, then a flight lieutenant, made the RAF his career and achieved 'Air' rank before retiring. This was one of the top four ranks in the RAF.

Other pilots came and went and I received my commission and moved to the officers' mess. I was now given a bank account and a cheque book, although at the outset I didn't even know how to write a cheque. Mess bills were required to be settled monthly (we signed chits for drinks in the bar) and not infrequently I had to go short, having spent my allowance and not being able to run up an overdraft. A few days after joining the officers' mess I came into the ante-room (fancy name for the lounge) where the group captain was sitting on the settee. He patted the seat beside him and said, 'Sit down and tell me about yourself.' At first I thought he liked very young officers in an unhealthy way but nothing untoward ever happened.

I had been to London to buy my officer's uniform from where I caught the train to Potters Bar to go to see my parents. I was walking from the station along Darkes Lane and feeling very self-conscious when a soldier who had been lounging against a shop window suddenly snapped to attention with sparks flying off the pavement from his hob-nailed boots and threw me a terrific salute. I just about remembered to return his salute, though he was obviously taking the Mickey out of this schoolboy-looking officer whose uniform almost crackled with newness. My parents were very amused by this.

To return to the Eagle Squadron, they had received orders to transfer to the south so the night before their departure they threw a mess party. This was so rough and noisy it probably recorded 5.9 on the Richter scale. After drinking toasts, the Americans all threw their glasses into the stone fireplace and they smashed. It did not occur to them that the glasses were quite irreplaceable and one could not ring up and get another set. Next day they decided to show off (a very unwise thing to do with a bad hangover) and took off twelve abreast. Somehow they all survived but not before the wing men on either side veered away untidily to make room for erratic flying of others inside them.

I made friends with a WAAF girl whose name, I think, was Esme. She declined my invitation to go into an air-raid shelter where it would be dark and private. She was probably wise not to put her virtue at risk, although little did she know that at that time I had no idea how to proceed to achieve seduction.

At Kirton there was a surprising event. One of the experienced pilots, whom I shall call Bob, was flying above cloud above Yorkshire, perhaps on a radar calibration exercise, when he was recalled and given a course to steer back to base. Flying on this course he descended and came out of the cloud only to find himself flying through the balloon barrage over Hull. This frightened him badly but he came through without having a wing sliced off by a balloon cable. His fright changed to extreme anger with the controller who had given a course which could have killed him. After landing he went down to the ops room (normally out of bounds) and, walking along the dais above the plotting board, he yanked the controller to his feet then seized the seat of his pants and threw him off the dais down onto the plotting board, which damaged both the controller and the plotting board. Bob was immediately put under close arrest in his room. A court martial was arranged.

Next morning all pilots were told over the PA system to report to dispersal at once and Bob, realising that a panic was on, put his flying gear on over his pyjamas and also reported for duty. The flight commander forgot Bob should not have been there and included him in the flight and the squadron departed to the south. (The occasion was when the German ships *Scharnhorst*, *Gneisnau* and *Prinz Eugen* made a daylight run through the channel catching the Royal Navy flat-footed.) The extra Spitfires were required to keep German fighters from attacking the few aged Swordfish torpedo bombers, which were all the navy could call on at the time.

The whole thing was a fiasco. The German ships shot down the torpedo bombers but some Spitfires and Messerschmitts did get into a fight. The squadron returned to Kirton, but without Bob, who was posted 'missing'.

Two days went past so Bob became 'lost in action' and arrangements for the court martial were cancelled.

On the third day a small aircraft landed and out stepped Bob, still damp from having spent two nights and days in his dinghy before being picked up and taken to Eastleigh, where he scarcely bothered to get dry and persuaded the pilot of the light aircraft to fly him back to Kirton. He was a very hardy man and he wound up his career flying intelligence people into France at night. Whether he survived, I do not know.

As is usual after being commissioned, I was posted away, this time to 154 Squadron at Fowlmere, a satellite of Duxford. It is much easier to arrive already as an officer than to become one in one's own unit when all one's friends suddenly have to address one as 'sir' instead of the previous 'Smithy'. The date was January 1942.

Before moving on to the story of my brief sojourn with 154 Squadron, I should mention some of the strange terms used, at least by fighter pilots and perhaps by aircrew in general. By this time I was using the jargon freely and thought nothing of it, although some of it must have baffled others. Among the terms most used were *shithot*, *prang* or *wizard prang*, *putting up a black*, *tearing off a strip*, *gash* and *press tits* (meaning start engines). There were no doubt others that I can no longer remember. Also certain types of operations had code names, the only one of which I can recall is 'rhubarb', which meant low-level hit-and-run raids. We used to do 'anti-rhubarb' patrols along the south coast to deter daylight bombing raids by German Focke Wolf 190 fighters, although we could not catch the 190s in a chase until the Typhoon came along. 154 Squadron operated Spitfire Mk. Vs. We had a commanding officer who never led the squadron but restricted his flying to an hour now and then on his own. Other than this he told us horrifying tales of life on the NW frontier of India. Sometime later I met another officer who had been there at the same time and he said most of it was tall tales.

There were outings from Fowlmere, mostly to Cambridge. I remember a pub called The Baron of Beef and another where the lounge area was placed in what originally had been a passage for stage coaches to drive through. No doubt these are still in business. It was usually some time after closing time before the transport came to pick us up and I used to stretch out on one of the market place tables and have a doze. I was rudely awakened one night when a complete stranger shook me and asked me 'did I know where George was'. To get rid of him I said, 'Go and look in the fountain.' This he did and much to his surprise, there was George. He came back and thanked me profusely, saying that George had fallen in and was too drunk to get out. In spite of my resentment at being woken, I could not help but laugh.

The intelligence officer of our unit was a young man who had been in the 'Golden Gloves' boxing team in international contests. His otherwise handsome features were spoiled somewhat by his flattened nose from which the bone had been removed. We also had a very well-built Canadian and after a disagreement they squared up to each other. We were hoping that they would come to blows, but after circling each other like a couple of tom cats, they decided to shake hands and we missed some entertainment. Also on the squadron we had a lone Frenchman wearing a French uniform. He spoke good English, but did not join in our rowdy behaviour. Whenever he managed to get a twenty-four-hour pass, he would pack a little case and walk out of the camp looking very smart. He never told us where he went on these occasions, but we presumed he had a girl somewhere quite close.

The flight commander was Flight Lieutenant Ronnie Fokes, with whom I was soon on the best of terms. He had his wife Audrey living in the village and on the airfield he was always accompanied by his dog, a white bull terrier and fortunately a friendly beast. One day he tied the dog to the inside of the van he used to run about in, but the lead was too long and the dog jumped out. Not noticing this, Ronnie started up and drove through the village to his home. When he got there he heard the dog whining and when he took him inside found he was missing quite a lot of skin and hair but as amiable as ever. No sense, no feeling, perhaps.

We did the usual things of practising formation flying, cine gun attacks, firing at targets in the North Sea, etc. We had a scramble or two leading to nothing, but on one occasion it really was serious. We flew from the east coast towards Holland and came across three motor gunboats. You can't tell from the air whether they are ours or theirs, so we circled around for a minute or two, holding our fire as the boats held theirs. Then Ronnie Fokes, who was the leader, made a very low pass close to the boats and said they were ours, after which he sent one section off close to the Dutch coast, attracting a little flak but confirming that the Germans were not in pursuit with their own aircraft or boats. We then all circled the boats until another squadron flew out to relieve us.

The story we were told was that one of our destroyers plus several gunboats went close to the Dutch coast at night. The destroyer was, of course, head on to the land and probably in line with a buoy to give little radar response. The gunboats then roared up and down the coast to entice out the German E-boats and when they put in an appearance our gunboats led them past the destroyer with its guns, which sank some E-boats and captured one. No doubt feeling cock-a-hoop they set off back to England with the captured E-boat in tow. The Germans, however, were not having this and sent out every available E-boat, which came in at forty knots, torpedoed and sank the destroyer and sank some of our gunboats with gunfire before recapturing their E-boat. The three boats we patrolled over were the sole survivors of this expedition.

Returning from this patrol our leader decided to land at Coltishall in Norfolk because fuel was running out for our return to Fowlmere. I noticed that my No. 2 was flying much too close to me. When I gave a blast of power to get me safely over the fence round the airfield, my slipstream caused my No. 2 to bounce violently off the ground and he had to open his throttle so as not to stall. In the meantime I had landed and, glancing in my mirror, I was appalled to see my No. 2 about fifteen feet above me, threatening to land on top of me. He could not see me at all. So I speeded up my taxiing, hoping that whoever was in front of me saw me coming and either got out of my way or speeded up himself. Another glance in the mirror showed that my No. 2 was safely on the ground, but we had a few words once outside our aircraft.

Ronnie Fokes was posted to Duxford to join the first squadron of Typhoons being formed there. Duxford station was having an exercise in protecting the airfield against ground attack one day. I went over earlier in the day, found Ronnie and he gave me a run-down on these ugly but fierce-looking aircraft. What a contrast to the elegant and graceful Spitfire, but they were later to have their day and what I learned about them that day helped me later on when one I was flying tried to dive me into the ground.

I was press-ganged into being an umpire in the pseudo-attack on the airfield. I found it hopeless as a very young officer to get assorted soldiers to agree that they had just been killed. When I attempted to lock them into a Nissen hut they burst out of the door the other end to join in the action again. I spent a miserable afternoon getting frozen stiff and once it began to get dark I slipped away back to the officers' mess. There was nobody about and I went into the kitchen to find something to eat and found a lot of roasted pigeons which I tucked into. Presumably someone had to go without that evening but by then I was back in the mess at Fowlmere and gave no thought to it.

My stay at Fowlmere came to an abrupt end in the middle of March and it was entirely my own fault. One evening four of us piled into someone's old banger and went out drinking. We must have really put it away because on our return we roared through the village yelling like savages and firing our revolvers in the air. This made the natives restless, as the saying goes, and not unnaturally they complained of our bad behaviour. Within twenty-four hours we were all posted away to different places and I landed up at 611 Squadron at Drem in Scotland. Once one had been posted, one's destination could not be divulged and, short of committing murder, one's sins could not catch up. The date was nearly the end of March 1942.

611 Squadron had as CO Squadron Leader Watkins, a Battle of Britain pilot with a DFC and he had acquired the nick-name of 'Dirty', of which I am sure he was unaware. I can only suppose this nickname was because he was invariably immaculate, with a very public-school accent and, as far as I know, he was a gentleman without blemish. It is just possible that my memory is totally at fault and that the nickname belonged to someone of a lower grade altogether.

The airfield at Drem was of grass but it did have a flare-path, with the electric wires being buried only a few inches deep. In common with RAF practice, tall poles were at both ends and each side of the flare-path. These poles were about ten feer high with a vertical row of lights nearer the top, what we called 'totem poles'. This was to make take-off and landing easier than following the very dim flare-path lights. This was particularly the case when the wind was not blowing dead down the flare-path and the pilot was obliged to 'crab' his approach in order to keep in line and then, putting on rudder at the last moment, to land in line and so prevent damage or even destruction of the undercarriage. You can see airliners doing exactly the same today.

Our flying was much the same as with previous squadrons, with scrambles at times, none of which led to anything, although we did intercept a Halifax bomber which must have had its IFF (Identification Friend or Foe) switched off, as ground control had taken it as a German. One day I was patrolling the Firth of Forth alone for some reason (a pair was the usual patrol), guarding HMS *Nelson* coming out of Rosyth. I flew on the seaward side because, if there was to be an attack, that is where it would be from. Nothing untoward happened for an hour then this mighty battleship had a practice shoot with all guns naturally pointing away from the shore, which was where I was. Presumably they took care not to shoot me down but they came close enough to frighten me badly and I hastily moved to the shore side for the rest of the patrol. I could imagine the Captain saying, 'Never mind that bloody Spitfire, test all guns.'

It was very important to have your teeth in full working order without any loose fillings. While flying at Drem I had been on a routine height climb and when descending at high speed I had the most piercing pain I my jaw. It was so bad that I screamed and held my face. Fortunately I had enough sense to climb up again and then descend more slowly. This worked but I lost no time in having the loose filling made good.

On 611 Squadron, there were two young Americans from the 'deep south' of the USA. Very mistakenly some of us, including myself, started to play poker with them. They rapidly relieved us of all our money and I, for one, resolved never to play poker again with Americans.

One of the other officers, slightly senior to me, was a big-head and loved to throw his weight around when the flight commander was not around to keep him in line. He also refrained in my presence because I would tell him to shut up. I went on leave and on my return some of the junior pilots came up and said, 'Thank God you're back.' The big-head had been making their lives hell in my absence.

While at Drem the squadron was scrambled to a rearward base as a practice against invasion. We landed at a bomber training unit and then the weather closed in and we were stuck there for several days without any clean clothes, shaving gear or money. It was miserable, although the CO opened credit for us in the mess bar on his own risk that we would eventually repay him. Some of the service women seemed to think that the fighter pilots were really something and acted like idiots in consequence, in spite of the fact that bomber crews had an infinitely worse time than we ever did. After our return from the bomber station we were chatting in the mess one evening and one of the company was an army officer, permanently stationed at Drem, whose job it was to arrange the defence of the camp against the enemy. Someone remarked that it was just as well our ground crews had not been sent after us by road or they would have been in a worse state than we were. The army officer then said, 'I would not have let them go.'

I said, 'What do you mean, you wouldn't have let them go? We can't fly without them.' He said that wasn't his responsibility and we were appalled by his narrow thinking, but as an airfield near the Firth of Forth was most unlikely to receive attention from the *Wehrmacht* we let the matter drop.

While on the subject of the army, the squadron was given the task of shooting up some trenches they had dug near the coast while the troops crouched down in the bottom. This was to give them some experience of being under fire and we had a good time doing it. The lone Frenchman in the squadron had trouble getting his engine to start and arrived over the trenches just after we had left. He then attacked the trenches from the other direction for some reason. We had no reports of casualties but, if there had been, the Frenchman would probably have given his best Gallic shrug of the shoulder and said, 'C'est la guerre.' We called him 'General' with a French pronunciation and he was a most amusing man, given to telling tall stories. One of these that I remember was his claim that, while taking off at night, he failed to check his Spitfire from swinging left so he was at an angle to the flare-path and having to fly up the slope. In doing so he said he had flown through a 'blister' hangar. This is very unlikely but it is just possible, so we never knew whether he was telling the truth or not.

Reverting to the subject of 'totem poles', these were normally of fragile construction so that if an aircraft hit one it was the pole that was broken and not the aircraft. This philosophy had no attraction to the Scottish clerk of works. No one was going to knock his lights over, so he made them out of nine-inch square baulks of oak set in concrete. As it happened our dispersal hut was quite close to one end of the flare-path and I was showing off one day doing a 'falling leaf' approach, which looks very pretty if done well. I could see one totem pole but lost sight of the other as I did the last sideways slide before straightening out to land. Then there was a loud crack and a jerk in the aircraft and I knew at once that I had hit the other totem pole and lost my left-side wheel. There did not seem any point in going round again so I landed on the right-hand wheel, which was easy enough with a narrow undercarriage like the Spitfire's, but as the aircraft slowed down the wing, without a wheel, eventually dug into the ground. The aircraft spun round and stood on its nose, smashing the propeller. The fire engine and the ambulance charged across the airfield and men pulled the tail down so I could get out. I was delivered to the medical officer for a check-up and the aircraft was lifted away. It was never the practice to make a pilot fly again immediately after a crash unlike in the First World War.

After my visit to the MO I went back to the mess where I found a furious Wing Commander Peter Townsend, who called me several sorts of bloody fool and ordered me to report to him next morning with my logbook. This I did and he endorsed the book saying 'Carelessness – failed to keep sharp look-out when coming in to land.' It might have been worse but for Townsend himself going up in a Tiger Moth aircraft to show off to a girlfriend and coming back with chicken wire round the undercarriage (he must have scared hell out of the chickens) so perhaps he could not be so hard on me. What he did do, I am sure, was to say to my CO, 'The next time a list comes up for posting somewhere dangerous put Smith's name on it.' I don't think Squadron Leader Watkins would have willingly posted me away without being ordered to do so. As it was a few weeks later I was posted to Malta.

Before going abroad I inadvertently did a lot of damage to the flare-path at Drem. On an ordinary flight the tail-wheel fell off my aircraft, leaving a spike several inches long sticking down from the tail. I was quite unaware of this but, on landing the aircraft, slowed far sooner than normal. So I swung off the path to get out of the way quickly, but found that the aircraft wouldn't move, in spite of opening the throttle. As a Spitfire's engine quickly overheats on the ground, I switched off and got out to see what the trouble could be. I found that the steel spike, where the tail-wheel should have been, had pulled up all the wiring for one side of the flare-path. This had now caught round the spike and stopped the aircraft. I was not to blame for it, but for all this they must have been glad to see the back of me. I left 611 Squadron on 20 May 1942 and went on embarkation leave.

Chapter 8

En route to Malta

I received orders to present myself at Liverpool docks where, together with twenty-nine other pilots, I embarked on a fast (fourteen knots) merchant ship, which had twenty-four Spitfires in bits in the hold. The upper forward cargo space had been converted to accommodation cabins made of wood and the whole of it stank of fresh paint. We set sail at the end of May with a sloop and a corvette as escort and set off for Gibraltar without a convoy, going as fast as the ship could manage. A few days into the voyage the sloop started flashing signals, which of course we could read. The signals said, 'Altering course owing to U-boat information.' As one man we ran down the stairs, grabbed our Mae Wests and ran up again. We stood panting on the deck, when the captain came off the bridge and said, 'What do you silly buggers think you are doing?' We said that we had read the signal and the captain said it happened all the time. We felt very foolish and took off our Mae Wests and put them on our bunks again.

Once outside the three-mile limit whisky could be bought for 6/6 (33p) a bottle so we took advantage and got drunk. We had a gramophone in our quarters but after a very drunk pilot played the same record thirty-three times someone got up and broke it over his head. The rest of the trip was uneventful. The seas changed from the dull green of northern climes to an unbelievable bright blue as we moved closer to the tropics. Dolphins played around the bow and apart from the continued risk of torpedoes we enjoyed the warm sunshine.

The senior officer amongst us was a very pompous flight lieutenant, who strutted about on the bridge to which the rest of us had no access. The captain of the ship probably got sick of him with his airs and graces, but he and his officers treated us very well and we ate in the officers' dining room, that is after a bout of sea-sickness. Eating well is my answer to that affliction.

My main interest was in the engine room where I was amazed at the size of the three-storeys-high diesel engine. It developed something like 2,000 h.p. which a couple of Merlin engines could develop with ease. The difference of course was that the ship's engine would thump away for weeks, turning a solid propeller shaft about twelve inches diameter with several tons of propeller at the end of it. I walked down the prop shaft tunnel to the end where it went through a gland. I realised that, should we be torpedoed, I would be done for, so I beat a rapid retreat.

We talked to the ship's officers about the risks and ever present danger of being at sea during wartime, but they said that nothing would ever get them into an aircraft. They much preferred the risks they were accustomed to. Being below the water line, the engineers and crew in the engine room had very little chance of escape if a torpedo struck. The area would become flooded in a few minutes and only one or two men could expect to get up the ladder in time.

Upon our arrival at Gibraltar we disembarked. When we walked out of the dock we saw market stalls bulging with fruit of all kinds and we bought a load of it. After disembarkation, the officers were put into the Rock Hotel, which was very comfortable. While we lived comfortably in the hotel there was a fury of activity on the dockside where the crated Spitfires were lifted ashore, broken open and the parts assembled into aircraft again. They were then shipped out to the aircraft carrier *Eagle* and the guns were tested, firing into the bay. Each Spitfire was rolled into its parking position, which for the first ones looked very perilous as they were put at the very end of the flight deck, which sloped steeply down towards the stern. The wheel chocks were placed behind the wheels to prevent the aircraft rolling back into the water. As far as I remember the whole job took about seven days.

During this time we were all ejected from the hotel when all the senior naval officers in residence took exception to our noisy behaviour one night. The cause of this eviction was an American, Tex Spradly (who was the most timorous man I ever met and I could not understand why he joined a fighting force in another country) who became the worm that turned. He went after a man who had bullied him on the voyage. Tex was armed with two revolvers and he was pulling the triggers while pointing the guns at the bully. The latter leaped off the balcony into the shrubbery. Tex (who was very drunk) was yelling, 'I'll get the bastard' and charged off downstairs waving the revolvers and so out into the grounds, with all the rest of us following and cheering him on. I think he had one round in each gun, which he fired into the bushes, after which he gave up and was put to bed. The next morning we were ordered to get our kit outside the hotel, where we were put into trucks which took us down to the harbour and then on a motor boat out to the *Eagle*. It must have caused the junior naval officers a lot of trouble because they expected to give up their bunks for just one night on the voyage and there we were in residence for four nights.

The convoy set out on 8 June 1942 at 09.00 hours in brilliant sunshine. As far as I remember some of the escort vessels left Gibraltar first, then the *Eagle* with us and the Spitfires on board, then the rest of the escort. The flotilla turned eastward through the straits and fell into sailing formation. It was a wonderful sight with all this naval hardware and every ship bristling

A tropicalised Spitfire Mk.VB being assembled at Gibraltar in 1942

A Spitfire Mk.VB taking off from an aircraft carrier in 1942

with guns including our carrier. To add some excitement a 'flak' cruiser that had been doing a work-out in the eastern Med came tearing towards us flat-out. A naval officer said that its station was twenty cables astern of us.

The captain of the 'flak' cruiser sent his ship into a turn and, heeling right over with a tremendous bow-wave, sliced through the escort, slowed down and pulled in twenty cables behind us. What a seaman their captain must have been.

The term 'flak' cruiser (the navy may have had another name) referred to their modified gun turrets which allowed the guns to be elevated much higher than normal and thus be able to fire at attacking aircraft. Altogether I think we had over a dozen powerful escorts of cruisers and destroyers, and submarines were lurking further east. The voyage was without incident and by full daylight next day we were approximately due north of Algiers when the zigzag course we had been following had to straighten to allow us to take off. Steering straight ahead was the period when all the navy was on tenterhooks in case an enemy submarine happened to get itself in a position to launch torpedoes, which is what happened to the *Eagle* and the *Furious* only a little later.

The aircraft we were to fly were tropicalised Spitfire Mark VBs, which were fitted with two 20mm cannon and four ordinary machine guns. The density of the fire from the cannons was only a fraction of that of machine guns, but with alternate rounds of armour-piercing and explosive shells the effect was lethal when an enemy aircraft was hit. The other features were the fitting of a thirty-gallon large belly tank, which could be jettisoned when empty, and a big filter in the air-intake to stop corrosive limestone dust from getting into the cylinders. This filter substantially reduced our top speed and also the ceiling at which we could operate. The enemy operated from hard airfields in Sicily and had no need of air filters and thus had an advantage over us in these respects.

We took off in rapid succession taking care not to let our Spitfires swing to the left, which they always tended to do unless corrected. It was absolutely necessary to keep the aircraft on the centre line, because the old *Eagle* had a pointed flight deck and if one ran off it to one side there was a terrific up-draught which could tip the aircraft over unless the pilot was very quick. The navy had twigged this in the early days and the centre line was painted about ten feet to the right so you could see it from the cockpit, which would not have been the case had it been painted down the centre.

We took off on main petrol tanks then changed to the belly tank at a safe height. If the belly tank failed to work, one was offered the alternatives of trying to land again on the carrier (virtually suicide on a small carrier like the *Eagle* because if one ran off the front of the deck the ship ran over you) or to ditch in the sea and wait to be picked up or to bale out and likewise be picked up. None of us had a failure but it is interesting that when a big USA carrier had made a couple of Malta runs, a Spitfire did land back on and the Admiralty realised that a top-class fighter could be used on larger carriers and development of the naval Seafire began. It was never a match for the land-based Spitfire because of the weight of extra-strength undercarriage and 'arrestor-hook' mechanism, which caught in wires stretched across the deck when landing.

We formed up in a loose formation at a height I cannot remember, but this would be between 15,000 and 20,000 feet. After flying due east for a spell, we turned south-east to cross over French Tunisia at Bizerta and Cape Bon to keep well clear of the small Italian island of Patelleria where there was a fighter airfield. We then flew east again to Malta, having jettisoned our belly tanks over Tunisia and hoping that some of them hit enemy property or people. After three and a half hours we reached Malta and the formation split up with each part to land at one of the three airfields: Takali in the west, Luqa in the centre and Halfar in the east. My airfield was Takali and the group landed safely, except for one pilot (who should have known better) who went off the end of the airfield and through a stone wall to crash his aircraft. The wing commander would have shot him on the spot if he could. About fifteen minutes after we landed, the Germans raided Takali and another new arrival was smashed. There were smashed aircraft and bomb craters all over the place and it certainly looked like a severely contested battlefield, as subsequent experience showed it to be. The most notable aircraft wreck was a 'Maryland' twin-engined bomber of which only the front end remained. Having no rear end it was tilted steeply back with its nose and engines pointing forlornly at the sky.

On landing, each aircraft was refuelled by using four-gallon tins of petrol poured in through a funnel. As an empty Spitfire would take twenty-two tins, it became a lengthy business. After this the aircraft were handed over to 'Malta' pilots to be in 'readiness' straight away. We were collected by lorry and taken to our quarters in M'dina, a holy city with high walls. At a subsequent briefing the wing commander (a savage man if ever there was one) told us that if we lost Malta we would lose the whole Middle East because from Malta naval aircraft flew to sink the bulk of supply ships to Rommel's Afrika Korps, with particular reference to fuel tankers. While the wing commander was speaking, a noisy altercation started in the street outside. The local police arrived and the wing commander opened a window and bellowed, 'Get those black bastards out of here.' This was a gross insult to the Maltese, but the crowd dispersed.

Chapter 9

Operations in Malta

The squadron I joined was at that time No. 603, as a result I suppose of 603 squadron pilots having flown to Malta en bloc, and they of course called themselves 603. Squadron numbers, however, do not belong to air crews, who are transient, but to ground crews who are permanent. As there were no ground crews from 603 on the island our number changed to 229. The other squadron sharing Takali was 249. On the airfield there was a dispersal hut built of limestone blocks with field telephones and pilots' equipment. It was frequently knocked down but Maltese workmen simply put the blocks together again with the tin roof. The aircraft stood in pairs of anti-blast pens made of sandbags or petrol tins filled with earth. These of course were open at the front and narrowed down towards the back, where the walls changed at an angle to present a 90° angle at the back. There was also a sandbag wall down the middle of each pair. Full petrol tins were stacked against the outside of the 90° angle thus ensuring that if one stack caught fire it was unlikely to set off the other stack, which was several yards away round the angle.

We were on duty from mid-day to mid-day. Thus from mid-day we would be in readiness till dusk, then before dawn on the following day until mid-day again, after which we were off duty again for twenty-four hours. There were more pilots than aircraft so operations were not restricted at any one time. Going on readiness at mid-day was usually spent sitting on the ground underneath the aircraft wing for the sake of shade from the sun. Dinner was brought down at about 1 p.m. on a plate with a cover over it. The cover was lifted and a stab was made with a fork while the lid was dropped on again before too many of the myriad of flies got inside. The flies were a curse and the first job on dawn readiness was to run a closed hand down the telephone wires in the hut which were covered an inch thick all round with sleeping flies. The pile, then on the desk, was swept into a paper bag and burned; not that it seemed to make a difference, but we felt better for doing it.

My first readiness session was not auspicious. That day we were on 'cockpit' readiness, all strapped in and waiting to go. This could not be tolerated for long because of the heat. My mouth was dry with fear of what might be about to happen and so I looked around to try to keep my mind occupied. I saw a Spitfire approaching with a dead engine. It seemed to be

A tropicalised Spitfire Mk.VB in an anti-blast pen made of petrol tins filled with earth

Pilots of 229 Squadron, Malta. The author is 3rd from the left in the front row

making a good approach but the pilot (presumably wounded) lost control on the final turn and crashed upside down and burst into flames.

This was about twenty-five yards away to my right front. The unfired ammunition began exploding and I was uncomfortably close, but nothing came my way. As the fire died down, cockpit readiness was cancelled and I climbed out. I saw a group of Maltese workmen approaching the wreck, though what they could find that might be useful I didn't know. However, our chief went past me and delivered a terrific kick in the backside to one of the workmen and bawled out, 'F--k off, you thieving bastards.' They did. The smell of a burning aircraft is not pleasant and when it has a body in it, it is truly awful. What was left of the pilot was pulled out for proper burial and the wreckage pushed aside. This event was by no means unusual in Malta at the time. After this episode I was more nervous than ever but when the 'scrambles' came I was too occupied getting into the aircraft, starting up and taking off to do any worrying. After take-off, on the long climb up to intercept the enemy I used to talk to myself about 'not to worry, you'll be all right' and that sort of thing. I imagine many pilots did the same.

Shortly after arriving in Malta I saw three groundcrew, two of whom were each holding one blade of a propeller, while the third was beating out the bent third blade. This would have given a UK engineering officer a bad case of post-traumatic stress disorder, had it been invented then. Blades can be straightened quite safely given appropriate heat treatment, but of course this was not available in Malta. I was not too keen on the idea of having to fly behind that propeller, but it came to no harm that I was aware of.

At dusk we walked up the road to M'dina for an evening meal (such as it was). A Maltese workman driving a truck used to pass us without offering a lift. So one evening we stood across the road so he had to stop. Our flight commander drew his revolver and pointed it at the driver's face and told him he ought to pick us up. This he did, of course, but managed to evade us by leaving early thereafter.

Walking down for dawn readiness in the dark was not much fun. If there had been a raid on Takali during the night, the Germans would almost certainly have dropped their 'butterfly' anti-personnel bombs. If one was kicked, the kicker certainly lost his leg, if not his life. I cannot understand why we did not take the elementary precaution of going single file while walking. On the airfield we could not fly until a couple of armoured cars joined by twenty yards of steel chain had driven down the airfield to explode any 'butterflies' littering the ground. The small craters had then to be filled in so aircraft wheels did not drop into them.

There were scrambles every day, often to no purpose. When we chased the Me 109s half way to Sicily, they were too fast for us and likewise the Italian Macchi 202 fighters when fitted with German engines. A lot of the daylight bombing was carried out by Italian bombers made of plywood. The first time I fired my guns in anger was on 23 June when I got a share in destroying an Italian bomber. Our flight commander was shot down that day but was rescued unhurt. On many occasions radar detected a build-up of aircraft over Sicily, which was only fifteen minutes flight away. We were scrambled to get as much height as possible at full throttle only to find the enemy formation had dispersed. This of course was only a ruse to get us to use our fuel supplies.

On one scramble I noticed, as I climbed onto the wing to get into the cockpit, that the perspex hood was wired on so that it could not be jettisoned. There was no time to argue about it then but when I landed and came back to the anti-blast pen I got hold of the mechanic and asked him very angrily why the hood was wired on. He said, 'We're getting short of hoods, sir.' This was one of the rare occasions that I really blew up and shouted did he 'expect me to sit in the cockpit and burn to death if I was hit' because he was 'short of bloody hoods?' (The Spitfire cockpit cannot be slid back other than at a slow flying speed.) He was to 'get a pair of pliers and cut the wire off' while I watched him do it. To be fair he may not have realised that the hood could not be opened at speed, but to do such a thing off his own bat was unforgivable.

Early in July we were scrambled to tackle the enemy's fighter escort to give other squadrons a chance at the bombers without fighter interference. When we made contact a free fight (plane against plane) developed. I had noticed, on our climb up, three Macchi 202s circling a little way off enjoying a grandstand view of the Spitfires and Me 109s trying to kill one another. I thought something silly like 'We can't have that, can we?' and being well fired up and therefore reckless, I flew straight at them. I could see they had German engines and should have thought better of it, but recklessness prevailed and so I kept going.

With casual ease, they simply climbed out of my way. My momentum gained me perhaps 300 feet but they went up 500 feet. Trying to reach them put my Spitfire in incipient stall, shuddering violently. I was screaming and shaking my fist at them but they kept well clear of this crazy Brit in his staggering aircraft. Realising at last that I could not reach them I levelled off and then saw a Me 109 a little below me, so I dived to get a shot at it. A precautionary look in my mirror showed the Italians after me in a flash with their superior power and the first one was already firing. My hot-headed recklessness changed to cold fear in an instant as I realised that once they decided to make a fight of it, I could not possibly survive an encounter with these three at that height. As I turned into the attack there was a bang somewhere in the fuselage confirming my fears so I rolled over on my back and went down vertically at full throttle in a tight spiral. The trouble with this was that in a few seconds I was going faster than any Spitfire was designed to go. So I throttled back, stopped the spiral and, looking out, saw that the ailerons were standing up showing the danger line (a peculiarity of the Spitfire which could lead to aileron reversal and could tear the aileron off and part of the wing with it). Making sure that the aircraft was level across the span of the wings, I started to pull out of the dive and blacked out at once. Normally a black-out will last 4–5 seconds but this must have been 8–10 seconds. Fortunately, the lateral stability of the Spitfire ensured that it stayed level and when I eased off pulling on the stick my sight came back and I was about 2,000 feet over the island. I went back to Takali and claimed that I had been hit but the bang proved to be a small hatch that had opened and banged against the fuselage. My escape was due to the lousy shooting of an Italian.

On 4 July we scrambled again to attack Italian bombers, one of which I damaged before getting into a dogfight, but then did not come close enough to an enemy aircraft to open fire. When this broke up I was surprised to see a Me 109 flying straight and level toward Sicily at 1,000 feet. The pilot must have been crazy or injured. I dropped below him where he couldn't see me and chased after him as he was not going very fast. When I got within 250 yards, I lifted the nose and fired at him. There were some bright flashes where my explosive shells hit, then the aircraft rolled over on its back and plunged into the sea. I should have had two more kills, but when I started firing at a Ju 88, another Spitfire came from underneath me only a few feet below so I had to break off my attack and pull the nose up to avoid chopping his tail off. This put me right in front of two Me 109s which I knew would be there and so I broke away to the right but not before one German hit the rear tail of my aircraft with a lot of bullets, which fortunately hit nothing vital.

On yet another occasion I caught another Me 109 flying back to Sicily but when I pressed the firing button only one cannon fired. This had the effect of slewing the Spitfire about twenty degrees to one side and before I could judge opposite rudder to keep straight, but I ran out of ammunition, and so a very lucky German went home to his tea.

I think it was when I was returning from this episode that I saw a German aircraft going down and shortly afterwards spotted a parachute. This was blown a little out to sea and a boat set out to pick up the pilot. There had been rumours that some Maltese boatmen picking up enemy aircrew had pulled them out of the water, robbed them of any valuables, then killed them and put them back in the water. I had no idea whether there was any truth in this, but I circled around while the German was rescued and saw the boat return to the coast. If the boatmen were tempted to do anything really nasty they knew I would report the incident and would not dare to come back without the one they had picked up.

As the strength of bombing attacks built up it became apparent that 249 Squadron, with which we shared Takali airfield, was scoring kills at a higher rate than we were. This was, I think, partly because the 249 Squadron CO, the very experienced Squadron Leader 'Laddie' Lucas, was a better leader than our CO, partly because, when those of us who had flown in the latest batch of Spitfires were shared out between the two squadrons, 249 Squadron collected a Canadian NCO called George Buerling. He was totally undisciplined and squadrons at home had been glad to be rid of him. He acquired the nick name of 'Screwball'. Malta was just the sort of place for such a pilot to shine. His flying was perfect and he was a dead shot from any angle. He opened his account by shooting down eight of the enemy in three days. He had calculated the exact amount of 'deflection' (i.e. the amount of aiming in front of the enemy to allow for his speed) according to the angle he approached from and this he had stored in his head. Three to four seconds of firing was all he needed to shred an enemy fighter. He needed looking after because it never occurred to him to check that there might not be an enemy on his tail and his very unselfish flight commander saw to it that his tail was always covered. I believe he destroyed over thirty of the enemy during his stay in Malta. Strangely he was killed after the war in an aircraft accident in Italy while on his way to offer his lethal talents to the Israeli Air Force.

If Takali was put out of action due to bomb craters on the landing strip, we had to land at Luqa and wait until the damage at Takali had been repaired. This only happened once, but on another occasion a big build-up began over Sicily and we were scrambled. Nothing happened so we landed again and in the midst of refuelling a small formation of Ju 88s hit the airfield. We dived into a stone-built surface shelter and crouched down. The noise of sticks of bombs exploding a few yards away was deafening and when we emerged one stack of fuel tins was blazing away. The aircraft I had just come down in had been hit by flying sandbags so the fuselage was bent and it was a write-off except for spares.

There was an amusing end even to this incident. An airman was ferreting around in the dust and rubble and suddenly gave a shout of joy. He had found the piece of bread he had been about to eat. In spite of a lot of dust on it, he stuck it on the end of a bayonet and toasted it on an almost red-hot sandbag and enjoyed the result. A strange result of this raid was that while we crouched in the air-raid shelter, we were all smoking, but afterwards we found that all our cigarettes had gone out.

In Malta too much happened to record it all, but there are a few incidents which stand out in my mind.

In the corner of the airfield there was a Beaufighter, a twin-engined night fighter, under camouflage netting. I got to know the pilot and when he said he was going up on an air-test I asked if I could go with him. He said it was OK and so after he climbed up into the seat I climbed in afterwards.

He shut the hatch and I stood on it looking over his shoulder. It was just before dark. He took off and after a few minutes I was freezing cold even though I don't think he went over 500 feet. There must have been ventilation somewhere, but of course the pilot had his warm jacket on. I was lucky that the pilot was not sent off on an interception at height. Subsequently a German raid hit the Beaufighter fair and square on the ground and it burnt so fiercely that part of the aircraft's duralumin skin caught fire. It burnt with a searing white flame like magnesium does and made quite a show. But it was an aircraft that we could not afford to lose.

The officers' mess was in a small building forming one side of a square. There were stone steps up to the first floor. Then, at right angles to these, another set of stone steps led up to the bastion on top of the enormous town walls. On our twenty-four hours off we often spent time up there watching enemy bombers plastering various parts of the island. One group of these came in from the west obviously heading for our airfield at Takali. A very accurate salvo of our flak guns burst close to the German formation leader and this caused him to veer sharply to the right so that his formation was coming towards the town. Someone said, 'Where is he going now?' and someone else said, 'Christ, he's coming here.' With one accord about two dozen of us tore down the steps into the building and I resolved to get under the snooker table. There were, however, already an unbelievable number of thrashing bodies under it and so I went down to the ground floor about three steps at a time then crouched under the steps. The bombs landed a few yards from the base of the town wall, which made a lot of noise but no damage was done.

Every so often pilots were given local leave, which was usually spent at a 'rest' hotel at St Paul's Bay. When I was given a forty-eight-hour pass I didn't feel like mixing it with a lot of other pilots and when coming out of the mess in the morning I saw the adjutant's bicycle leaning against the wall. On impulse I took it and rode away, thinking that the adjutant could walk to the base for a couple of days as we had to all the time. I had a wonderful sense of freedom and of safety. No one was going to say me nay and no one was going to shoot at me for forty-eight hours.

I rode to the south of the island and came across a small radio repeater station with a staff of one NCO and a few airmen, sufficient to man the station twenty-four hours per day. They were delighted to see a new face for a change. We ignored the niceties of rank while they put before me a large bowl of thick soup made from dried lentils which I thought was delicious and said so. They did not agree, having had to exist on lentils in between visits of the ration truck. I wondered how it was that this isolated unit wound up with a shed full of dried lentils, probably the whole stock on Malta. I think they lent me some swimming trunks and a towel and I rode down to the beach for a swim, getting stung by a jelly fish, but not bad enough to cause the dreadful open sores some jelly-stung people suffered. I assume that I stayed on a spare bed that night and after more lentils for breakfast cycled off, riding around the little lanes and arriving back in the mess in mid-afternoon. I put the cycle back where I had found it. While nobody had seen me take it or put it back, obviously its absence coincided with mine and the adjutant had words to say. These I cannot remember but I gathered that, short of shooting the wing commander, the most heinous crime a junior officer could commit was to deprive the adjutant of his bicycle. Water off a duck's back to me.

Towards the end of July pilots with experience of flying Hurricanes were invited to volunteer for night-time dive-bombing attacks on enemy airfields in Sicily. I volunteered at once, not from a sudden rush of bravery but because I really would have liked to give the enemy a little of his own medicine and because I liked flying at night with just the glow from the instruments and sometimes the stars for company, a sensation I greatly enjoyed. I was sent to Halfar at the eastern end of the island, where quarters were provided down in the town. It was suffocatingly hot and humid and Halfar airfield itself was heavily raided that night with a few bombs falling in the town.

At breakfast next morning I was sitting opposite one of the other Hurricane pilots when a wing commander came in and sat at the head of the table. The steward brought in his breakfast with a rack of toast and a pot of real marmalade. We just sat and chatted while I hoped against hope that he would leave some of his toast, which indeed he did. As soon as he left, we grabbed the slices and liberally laid his marmalade on and ate them eagerly. I bet he was annoyed next morning to find that nearly all his marmalade had gone missing.

After breakfast I walked up to the battered airfield and went into the HQ building, which had been hit during the night. One walked along spotless and polished lino, which ended on the edge of a bomb crater and then started again on the other side. A couple of other pilots and myself were told that the Hurricanes were bombed up and were waiting for the craters in the strip to be filled in. When this was done we took off one at a time to fly to Luqa where we could use the flare path at night. Unfortunately I had completely forgotten that the nose of a Hurricane slopes down more than the Spitfire. When I tried to land, I stalled the aircraft at ten feet and fell with an awful crash onto the runway. The bombs fell off and rolled away. When I shamefacedly presented myself to the wing commander he said, 'Thanks for volunteering but if that is what you do to a Hurricane in daylight I cannot let you fly one at night.' I said, 'No, Sir', saluted and left his office. I went to the mess and asked for breakfast and, as no one knew I had already had one, another was served, after which it was back to Takali.

At this time we were getting desperately short of serviceable aircraft. One day the flight commander came into the dispersal hut and said there was a delayed action bomb under a Spitfire about a hundred yards away and someone had to go and taxi it to safety. An argument broke out about how we were to draw lots for this dangerous duty. I thought the bomb might well go off before the argument was settled and we just *had* to save the aircraft. I said I would go and so I ran out and told the duty despatch rider to take me to the aircraft. This he did and as soon as my feet touched the ground he shot out from between my legs going at full throttle to safety, which left me feeling a bit lonely with a Spitfire and a small hole in the ground with the bomb in it.

Having committed myself, I was quite calm and walked round the aircraft to climb in. The starting procedure had to be just right because the on-board battery would turn twenty-seven litres of Merlin engine only about one revolution. After priming the engine I pressed the two red buttons and after about one quarter turn the engine fired and I let off the brakes and taxied out over the bomb. It could not have been more than five seconds later that the bomb exploded and lumps of rock went flying all around. By reflex action I slammed the hood shut. Not that it would have kept out a large piece of rock but certainly cricket-ball sized pieces which otherwise would knock me unconscious. Actually not a piece touched me or the aircraft. A very lucky escape.

On 29 July four of us were scrambled to intercept a low-flying enemy aircraft, which proved to be an Italian sea-plane. Upon our approach it landed and a man climbed out on the wing and waved his white shirt. Our section leader reported this on the radio and we flew around until we saw a boat coming out to tow it in. It contained the crew of one of our torpedo bombers, which had come down in the sea close to Sicily. They had been rescued and put on the sea-plane to be flown to Taranto for questioning, with an Italian pilot and a soldier as guard. The soldier obligingly fell asleep, so the bomber pilot snatched his rifle while the crew sat on the soldier. Then he stuck the rifle in the pilot's ribs and said, 'Malta' and pointed south. The pilot obliged and that is when we saw them. Subsequently our wing commander took it upon himself to go and fly this seaplane. He told no one, but when he was airborne he showed on the radar and another scramble took place. By the greatest luck for the wing commander (which he little deserved) the section leader's windshield was badly oiled up (a frequent problem in the heat) so he shot at the blur, which was all he could see. He had to land in a hurry and was seen taxiing at speed back to Valletta harbour.

Analysing my short period in Malta, it was surprising that so much of it was a waste of time and petrol. From my first scramble on 17 June to the end of that month there was only six scrambles and on three of those we saw nothing. On two of these Me 109s were chased towards Sicily, but they were too fast for us and on another I did get a share of shooting down an Italian bomber. In July there was a dramatic change of pace with two or three scrambles each day. As we were on readiness for half a day at a time, three scrambles meant only time to rearm and refuel before going off again. I have no entries for 3, 7, 17 and 18 July. From 21 to 27 July I have no record. This presumably was when I had my forty-eight hours' leave and perhaps a dose of tummy upset afterwards.

Out of a total of thirty-one scrambles, thirteen led to nothing at all. On several others we were jumped by enemy fighters, largely because we were denied a high rate of climb due to fuel shortages so we had to try to intercept from underneath. Engine warm-up time was kept to a couple for minutes for the same reason.

The arrival of the tanker *Ohio* on 5 August, and the delivery of another group of Spitfires just before, finally put paid to the ambition of putting Malta out of action. The Germans had withdrawn several hundred aircraft from the Russian front to do this and by the end of July had lost half of them. We had only a few Spitfires left (only three in our squadron, as far as I can remember) until this new flight arrived.

Towards the end of my short stay in Malta animal stock was being slaughtered as there was nothing with which to feed them. My room-mate managed to buy a chicken which had been killed and we asked the cook to boil it for us. It was an astonishingly tough bird but we stuck at it for over an hour and were finally sated, which made a wonderful change.

For sheer devotion to duty I have to cite a Maltese gentleman of small stature but carrying a large suitcase. He was the local representative of Gieves the Tailors of London. In spite of the heavy bombing, he travelled to every officers' mess the length and breadth of Malta, sometimes arriving on foot in an attempt to sell made-to-measure officers' uniforms. He turned up twice at our mess over a period of about six weeks, but how he covered the whole territory I don't know. If he survived, one hopes Gieves gave him at least a nice gold watch.

Apart from being hungry most of the time, which tempted people to buy fruit when there was any and which was the probable cause of many a bout of tummy trouble, there was not enough alcoholic drink to go round the hard-drinking aircrew. Supplies of local beer were frequently interrupted by bomb damage to the brewery and supplies of spirits were rapidly consumed. Locally-made sherry was sometimes available but caused dreadful hangovers. A local liquor called 'Ambeet' (that is how it was pronounced but probably spelt differently) was pretty poisonous stuff and we were strongly advised not to touch it. Soldiers, sailors and airmen visiting the 'Gut' in Valletta for drinks and women no doubt did drink it and managed to survive.

There was a civilian background, of course, to fighting in Malta. Foremost in my memory was the plethora of priests in M'dina, and probably in most parts of the island, which was strictly Catholic. They held complete sway over the local populace. We heard a story that when young couples were married and the girl did not get pregnant in short order, a priest would go and try to impregnate her himself. I found this difficult to believe of priests sworn to celibacy. We had been warned not to interfere with the priesthood in any way at all. However, there was one incident which was both comical and serious at the same time. A Canadian officer came into our ante-room one night, very drunk and carrying a large and over-ripe water melon. He looked at it and said, 'I don't want this goddamned thing' and then lobbed it out of the first floor window. Of course, it had to hit a passing priest who, after recovering from his initial shock, gave vent to loud shouts of outrage about being drenched in blood-red juice from the impact. I do not remember if there was any follow-up to this, except that the offending officer's billet was cleared and he was bundled into a van with his belongings and driven off somewhere else; all in about fifteen minutes.

Next door to our billet there lived a family of the Maltese aristocracy. Their large house was perched right on top of the old city walls. They had a bevy of beautiful daughters and three of the eldest used to come out onto the bastion in their silk pyjamas with us and watch the island receiving its usual battering with bombs. It was a case of 'look but don't touch'. Any attempt at any familiarity would book you for a shotgun wedding. The eldest girl did bring me some grapes when I was in hospital, which made the other occupants of the ward envious.

One evening an open-air cinema was put up in the town of Rabat, which joined onto M'dina where our officers' mess and lodgings were situated. A few of us went but did not stay, having seen the film at home. Furthermore, we were pestered by biting flies which did not settle on the skin where they could be brushed away, but settled on our long socks which we wore with khaki shorts. Then the fly would bite enthusiastically through to the skin, causing intense irritation. I suppose the local population were immune to these pests and, in any case, the cinema gave the locals a much needed escape from their dreary, hungry and dangerous lives in wartime Malta. I presume that the film unit travelled from town to town performing wherever there was no enemy action, which of course would oblige it to switch off.

All of us smoked and cigarettes were much prized. My room-mate and I had a good stock in our billet, but this started to vanish. My Canadian room-mate gave our little Maltese batman a beating because it seemed certain that he was the thief, in spite of his protestations of innocence. However, going back to our billet for something or other during one morning, our landlady who lived downstairs was found helping herself to our stock. So the Maltese boy suffered for her thievery.

What I hated most in Malta was the summer heat. The island is far from being the hottest area of wartime operations. I don't now how I would have coped with the furnace-like heat of Aden or the steam-bath heat of India or Burma, if I had been posted to such places.

My last flight in Malta was on 30 July, at which time I was beginning to feel really ill. My internal economy did not like the food and along with most other pilots I suffered bouts of extreme constipation and sessions of the runs, which we called the Malta dog, a close relative to Gippy tummy and Delhi belly. I was sent to Imtarfa hospital where hepatitis was diagnosed and I was fed on children's rusks and golden syrup. I was turned out long before full recovery to make room for seriously injured sailors from the August convoy of which only five ships survived. One of them was the tanker *Ohio* which came in lashed between two destroyers with its decks awash but with precious fuel aboard. Before leaving the hospital I was warned not to eat any fatty food or drink any alcohol. I totally ignored this well-meant advice and began to feel better. However, our CO said my health was not good enough for me to stay in Malta so on 24 August 1942 I was flown out with several others in a transport aircraft in one night-time hop to Gibraltar. One of the passengers was a naval officer who had lost a leg and he did not react to our attempts to talk to him.

After the privations of Malta (a relative term, aircrew had better rations than anyone else) the cornucopia of food and drink available at Gibraltar seemed beyond belief. In the five idle days I was there I put on several of the pounds that I had lost in Malta and felt fit again. At the end of five days in the transit officers' mess another night-time hop took us to Hendon. We took it in turns to keep watch out of the astrodome in the roof of the aircraft in case of attack from night fighters but, to everyone's relief, nothing untoward occurred. England looked lovely and all the girls looked likewise to my starved eyes. A good spell of leave was granted and on the form relating to my subsequent posting I asked to be posted back to 611 Squadron, then serving at Biggin Hill. To my delight this was granted.

I must tell the story of a pilot, in transit like myself, who met some naval officers drinking in a bar in Gibraltar. He was invited back to their wardroom where, no doubt, pink gin was imbibed. He was given a spare bunk to sleep on. When he awoke he was immediately aware that the ship was no longer tied up in Gib, but pitching and rolling as it proceeded to sea at high speed. He found out that the cruiser was going out into the Atlantic before turning north and zigzagging back to base in the UK. The navy had no use for passengers so he was put on deck with binoculars (along with many sailors) to watch for and identify any aircraft which came within sight. Presumably he was given some warmer clothing. The pilot probably consoled himself with the notion that he would be home in three days, but it was not to be. The cruiser came alongside a refuelling point for a few hours and then steamed off as escort to an Arctic convoy bound for Murmansk, with the RAF pilot having to do his stint. The cruiser, its crew and the sole RAF man present returned safely after something like three weeks. One imagines that the pilot avoided drinking with naval officers thereafter.

Chapter 10

Biggin Hill 611 Squadron

I STARTED FLYING with 611 Squadron in the third week of September 1942. The commanding officer was Squadron Leader Hugo Armstrong, who was an Aussie. He had brought a lot of other Aussies into the squadron. Later in my service at Biggin Hill he was shot down and lost, being replaced by Squadron Leader 'Wag' Haw. He was famed for his inability to fly from one place to another without getting lost, although he seemed to find his way round northern France and back to Biggin Hill, even if he did have to fly up the Brighton railway line to do it. The station commander was Group Captain 'Sailor' Malan, a super fit officer, but not to my liking. Not that this was the slightest consequence to him. No doubt he was disliked by many, in spite of his fine record during the Battle of Britain. He was South African and developed Parkinson's disease after returning there and he finally died of it.

During 1942 great strides had been made in the performance of fighter aircraft. This began when the Germans produced their new fighter, the Focke Wolf 190. This was a fine aircraft with a phenomenal performance that totally outclassed the Spitfire V. It had much greater speed in level flying and in climb and in dive. It could not stay in a tight turn with a Spitfire but its aileron control was so light that it could flick into turn before a Spitfire was even halfway in and so get a deflection shot before the tightness of the Spitfire's turn defeated it. It also maintained this performance for thousands of feet above what a Spitfire could reach and so was able to dive down out of the sun and claim its victims. The Spitfire Vs suffered greatly.

Rolls-Royce must already have been working on high altitude engines because it was not long before the Spitfire IXHF appeared in service and these were being flown by the Biggin Hill wing, including 611 Squadron. This aircraft had a slightly longer nose to allow a two-speed, two-stage supercharger to be put at the back of it and it was an injection engine, which meant it did not cut out in negative 'g'. The second speed and second stage of the supercharger came in just below 22,000 feet. The switch for it was left on 'manual' until the order came to go to the second speed, otherwise each aircraft would cut in at slightly different heights, causing disruption in the formation. Once the supercharger was operated, a cloud of black smoke came out of the exhausts and everyone throttled back. I believe the extra power was of the order of 500 h.p. and the aircraft could

611 Squadron at Biggin Hill, 1942–43. The author does not appear, being in bed with flu

IXHF Spitfires, 1942–43

IXHF Spitfires, 1942–43

IXHF Spitfires, 1942–43

then operate up to about 40,000 feet. This was enough to tackle the FW 190 and so its superiority lasted only a fairly short time. The Spitfire IX matched the FW 190 in every respect.

One of our pilots was an Irishman, nicknamed 'Paddy', of course. He was a very nice man, but a bit of a dream; what the Irish call being 'away with the fairies', I believe. On one high-level sweep, just before the squadron leader said, 'Second speed', Paddy's engine changed gear and he all but disappeared in his black smoke before he stopped daydreaming and turned back to join us again. He was teased about this, but his dreaming ultimately caught up with him. He was attacked from behind by a FW 190 and in spite of calls to him to 'break', he just flew on until he was shot down by the FW 190.

Some time later a lower level engine was developed with a smaller (or cropped) two-speed, two-stage supercharger (the IXLF) and it looked exactly like the HF model. It could climb straight off the ground at 5,000 feet per minute and the second speed came in at 12,000 feet. This restored the RAF's superiority at all levels and the FW 190 became very wary of tackling these aircraft. The old Spitfire problem of ailerons standing up dangerously at high speed had been cured by fitting a narrow turned-up flange to the trailing edge of the aileron, the downward thrust upon which prevented it from rising to an unsafe level. In due course one of these low-flying Spitfires was flown in for some of us to try it. It really was startling compared with the high-flying ones, which were not at their best at low level. The smaller supercharger, which took much less power from the engine to drive it, coupled with a new design of propeller, made it leap into the air and climb away like a rocket. I believe it was intended that 611 Squadron would be re-equipped with these in due course, but this did not happen during my service there.

Our job was two-fold: first to fly high-level fighter sweeps over northern France and second to escort US bombers, mainly USAF B17s, known as the 'Flying Fortresses', as far as we could go on our limited fuel. At this stage the Americans had no VHF radio intercom and had to borrow some from the RAF, which they soon replaced with their own mass-produced copy, which the RAF also used. They had naively assumed that their high operating level of about 30,000 feet and the massed machine-gun fire from a large formation would protect them. But the *Luftwaffe* attacked them head-on and then slipped away before the gunners could get any good shots. As soon as we were obliged to depart the *Luftwaffe* fell on them, and looking back I cannot imagine why we were not fitted with drop-tanks to provide another 20–30 minutes fighter cover. Details of these operations are set out below.

For bomber escort we flew at about 35,000 feet, which gave us the chance to 'bounce' (attack from above and behind) any FW 190s who dared to have a go at the bombers. Bomber crews liked to see their escort close by but it made it impossible for the escort to intercept attacking fighters and so, as often as not, the bomber crews could not even see their escorts. I think the USAF also thought that 30,000 feet took them out of 'flak' range but in fact the German 88 mm anti-aircraft gun could reach this height with ease. It is unbelievably cold at 35,000 feet and initially our aircraft were unheated. Subsequently a crude heating system of open-ended pipes welded into the exhaust stubs and discharging into the cockpit made it a bit more comfortable.

The USAF B17s were at this time restricted to fairly short-range attacks because their early long-range attacks on German targets had resulted in catastrophic losses which could not be sustained. Their range was extended a bit by the arrival of P47 Thunderbolt fighters, but even these could only escort the B17s to the German border.

The top brass in the USAF demanded fighters which could escort bombers to Berlin and back and they finally got these, courtesy of Rolls-Royce who had the idea of putting in the high altitude Merlin engine in the P51 fighter normally fitted with an Allison engine. This produced what can fairly be called 'the Allied fighter of the war'. Not only did it have enormous internal petrol capacity but could get off the ground with two extra drop tanks. The Merlin engine was copied by the Americans and produced in vast quantities. The Germans could hardly believe what they were seeing and even their jet fighters, the Me262, could not cope with hundreds of P51s. Even so the USAF lost 95,000 young airmen in their daylight bombing raids.

My first few flights were used for getting to know the type of aircraft and the local flying so that I got to know the sector. This was during the last few days of September. In early October I flew in a series of anti-rhubarb patrols. The chances of catching a fighter carrying a single bomb were remote on its run-in, as it would have dived all the way across the Channel at a great speed. There was just a chance on its way back but I never saw one. On 11 October I was part of a high-level fighter sweep over Hardelot to St Omer and back over Gravelines. The sky was empty. Other squadrons were sweeping over different areas, also without a response from the *Luftwaffe* as far as I know. Next day we formed a standing patrol over six destroyers on their way from one port to another.

An exercise for Army co-operation was flown on 15 October and on the same day there was a scramble but nothing happened. The next day I flew another fighter sweep, this time over Calais and Boulogne. Nothing was seen. There was another scramble later in the day, but it was only fifteen minutes until I was back on the ground again. On 21 October the whole squadron flew to Predannack on top of the cliffs in Cornwall, from where, after refuelling, we escorted B17s over the Cherbourg peninsula. Flak came up but no enemy aircraft were seen. We flew back to Biggin the same day.

I had a few flights over the next few days including one when I flew our flight commander to Hornchurch in a Tiger Moth and came back solo. It felt very strange to fly one of these again. There was a fighter sweep on 25 October but the squadron had to return due to bad weather. There were three anti-rhubarb patrols in November and three fighter sweeps. The first of these was to Hardelot, St Omer and out again at Gravelines. Our CO insisted on flying in four rows of three in 'vic' formation, being guarded from attack from the rear by an unfortunate 'arse-end Charlie' whose job it was to weave back and forth at the rear, rubber-necking to check no enemy was chasing us. Everyone else had long since given up this idea and flew the 'finger-four' formation, where those on the right kept their eyes on the sky to the left rear and vice versa. This formation gave thorough cover against being 'bounced'.

On 9 November, when I was arse-end Charlie, I did a left-hand sweep and then, as I came round to the right hand, I saw a FW 190 coming in at terrific speed already firing its guns. I yelled to the squadron to 'break right' which they did. I was already turning to the right so had time to get into a really tight turn before the FW 190 could get his sights on me. He missed the lot of us. Then my engine failed and lost all power and so I had to straighten up, whereupon the engine suddenly surged then faded again. By the time I had gone through 360° to get back on the track home, the squadron had disappeared. I had to make a choice between weaving back and forth to protect my own rear, which would certainly mean my doing a crash-landing in France, or flying as straight and level as my engine allowed in an effort to get back across the channel, but running the risk of an FW 190 coming up unseen and shooting me down. I chose the latter and after a while the engine settled into normal running and, as I approached the French coast, I saw a Spitfire coming towards me which proved to be the CO who had come back to see if he could find me. We flew back together to Biggin Hill.

The second patrol, on 10 November, was to cover the return of some bombers. Nothing was seen. The third, on 17 November, was aborted after about forty-five minutes due to a thick haze. A very difficult landing was made with a low sun on the haze making the airfield almost invisible. I got down by flying around the perimeter track at about 250 feet, down sun, and then abruptly doing a side-slipping tight turn round onto the runway as the end of it came into view. How all the others managed I do not know, but we all got down in one piece.

During December 1942 there was one fighter sweep and three escorting flights covering B17s. The sweep encountered 'bags of FW 190s', as it says in my logbook, but I did not get to fire at any of them, nor I believe did anyone else. I suppose the 190s made themselves scarce. The three escorting trips were long ones of about 1 hour 45 minutes, which leaves the Spitfire with very little fuel to get home on. The first escort job saw me landing at Detling for fuel and on the other two I landed at Ford for the same purpose. On the second of these there were a lot of FW 190s below us but we were high cover so presumably another wing at intermediate cover saw them off.

It was after landing from one of these three sweeps that I saw a civilian estate car standing outside our dispersal hut and the owner was handing out bottles of beer to the returning pilots. I had my bottle, which went down very nicely, thank you, then asked who this man was. The story given to me was that he was a surgeon who lived locally while working at a London hospital. He had the run of the camp and was an honorary member of the officers' mess. This was because of his great help during the attacks on the airfield in 1940 when he made a gadget that could detect the presence of large lumps of iron such as bombs buried in the ground, presumably by magnetic means. This meant that unexploded bombs could be located and marked on the surface and then subsequently dug out (a very scary job). The surgeon would then defuse the bombs (where he got his expertise from I have no idea) and remove the explosives, some of which he kept. Once loose it would not explode but could burn fiercely. With this explosive he undertook to remove a large tree growing out the side of the hill, the crown of which grew above the runway level. Some service men dug a hole under the tree and the surgeon poured in his store of explosive, inserted a fuse and had the hole back-filled and stamped down. Moving to what he thought was a safe distance, he lit the fuse and awaited events. He overdid it a bit and, after a stupendous explosion and all the rocks and clods of earth had stopped falling, there was a huge smoking crater and no tree. I do not know if it was found out where it went but I can vouch for the crater which some of us went to see.

The only fly in the ointment at Biggin was our impossible flight commander. He was the most unpleasant man it has ever been my misfortune to meet and he treated his pilots worse than a medieval lord of the manor would treat his lowest serfs. The effect on morale was disastrous in our flight. So another officer and myself made an official request to Squadron Leader Armstrong to have him removed. The flight commander screamed at the CO that he should not be listening to his subordinates and by doing so sealed his own fate. We never saw him again and another officer was promoted in his place. The only thing I remember about him, apart from the fact that he did a good job, was his nickname of 'Gin Bottle', but I don't think we used it where he might hear us.

I was standing in the hall in the officers' mess one day talking to some colleagues when I was suddenly faced by a man I recognised as the Minister for Air standing only a foot away. He barked at me, 'What do you think of the Spitfire IX then, heh?' I said 'Er, it is a great fighting aircraft, Sir, but not as pleasant to fly as the old Spitfire II.' I don't remember if he answered that. He was Sir Archibald Sinclair.

In January 1943 I record only one local flight lasting thirty minutes. I presume that the weather made operational flying too difficult and dangerous. On 5 February we flew an air sea rescue mission to try and find Squadron Leader Armstrong who had just been shot down, but no trace was found. His name appears at the Air Force memorial at Runnymede. He was replaced by Squadron Leader 'Wag' Haw, as noted at the start of the chapter. Until 14 February there was only practice flying, but on that day there was a scramble followed by a Channel patrol for one and a half hours. The next day I was in an operation as 'bouncing wing' above bombers. They could not find what they were looking for. Ground control broke down and so we came home having achieved nothing. On the same day we flew 'high cover' for some USAF Liberator bombers. There were no enemy aircraft but the flak was intense. I saw two bombers hit by flak. One of them had its port wing shot off outboard of the engines. The aircraft started gyrating madly round the missing wing, then diving down, still gyrating, all the way to the ground. No one baled out, presumably being pinned to the side of the aircraft by the violence of the spinning. On 17 February we flew as 'bouncing wing' again but the cloud was 10/10th and nothing was seen. Apart from a Channel patrol on 4 March, this was my last operation at Biggin Hill.

The squadron itself, of course, flew many more operations than just those in which I took part. There were plenty of pilots so that no one had to fly on every operation. For me this was noticeable towards the end of my time at Biggin, my flight commander having taken the view that I was getting stale. He was probably right for, although I faced the enemy only a fraction of the time that many others did, I had been operational since July 1941. Every scramble and every sweep held the prospect of mortal combat even if none materialised, except in Malta. For all that, I did not want to leave.

There were other items of interest. Biggin had a Blenheim bomber and an autogiro (ancestor of the helicopter), but I forget what their duties were. One of our smaller Aussie pilots was posted to an 'Aircobra' squadron. This strange single-seat fighter had the engine behind the pilot (not to be recommended in the event of a heavy crash-landing). The propeller shaft ran under the pilot's seat and between his legs. No one taller than five foot eight inches could get into it. It also had a dangerous tendency to topple end over end if mishandled. I do not know if recovery from this was possible. The only other unusual aircraft type at Biggin was the arrival of a 'Whirlwind' squadron for refuelling. This was a single-seat twin-engined fighter, heavily armed with four cannon and, I believe, two bombs carried externally. It was used, I think, in shipping strikes, an exceedingly dangerous business.

Other developments were taking place, the simplest of which being to abandon our matt-finish camouflage paint and have a high-gloss finish instead. The original reason for the matt-finish was to prevent the aircraft glinting in the sun but, as we were now seldom attacked, the gloss paint gave us a startling increase in top speed of about 25 mph. Another development was the installation of giro gun-sights. Apart from their much larger size the sight looked no different. But the centre spot was actually a double one, with a moving spot detaching itself from the centre when the aircraft moved from level flight. If you were attacking another aircraft there was no need to judge the deflection needed; you simply 'flew' the mobile spot (known as 'Willy') onto the aircraft you were going to shoot at. Then he would be hit, provided you were within range. The only problem with this sight was that it was so large that in a crash-landing the pilot was liable to smash his face on it in spite of being strapped in. This injury became know as 'giro-sight face' and some pilots suffered severely if they forgot to lock their harness back before making a crash-landing.

The most important development was the advent of 10 cm radar. Up to the time that this came in (spring 1943, I think) radar gave information about the direction in which enemy could be found but could not resolve the height/distance equation, because a small aircraft fifty miles away at 20,000 feet looked exactly the same on radar as a larger aircraft seventy-five miles away at 30,000 feet. The 10 cm radar could actually 'place' the enemy wherever he was with precise height, distance and his bearing from where we were flying. (This radar was also the basis of the Navy's success against U-boats.)

I wanted to bring my fiancée to Biggin for a mess party and asked the station admin officer if this was possible. He said that I must know that this was not permitted but I said that it was not to have her in my quarters but thought that the WAAF officers might have a spare bed. The station admin officer told me to ask Queen Bee (senior WAAF officer). So I did and she laid on a room and a batwoman and my fiancée enjoyed the unaccustomed luxury. The Queen Bee referred to above was a very distinguished lady and I believe stayed in the service to become OC of all WAAFs with a rank of group captain or even air commodore.

Attempts were made to get the Navy, Army and RAF to exchange officers. On offer were trips on convoys down the East Coast, which was avoided like the plague as being too bloody dangerous, or visits to army

The girl I fell in love with

camps. I applied for the latter and found myself in a muddy field with the 10th RTR with Churchill tanks. I thoroughly enjoyed myself and learned to drive their tanks. At dinner time on the first evening the gong sounded and the young army officers started a stampede into the dining room when their colonel said, 'Gentlemen, we have a guest today.' The officers stopped dead and the colonel ushered me into the dining room to sit next to him. All very proper and polite. The army came to stay with us but apart from meals and drinking in the evening there was nothing for them to do except to attend our operation briefings and debriefings. They soon got bored and were glad to go back.

Quite unexpectedly I had a phone call from my brother-in-law whose ship, a Hunt class destroyer, was in Sheerness for a refit after a long period sailing up and down the east coast, or E-boat alley, as it was called. He invited me to visit and so I obtained a forty-eight hour pass and travelled to Sheerness where a hotel room had been booked for me. I took a taxi to the destroyer and spent the evening in the wardroom drinking pink gin served by the wardroom steward while the young officers posed with their left hands tucked in their jackets *à la* Nelson, and a pink gin in the other. I became very drunk and had to be escorted to a taxi to get back to the hotel. The next day I invited the officers ashore to drink beer and they got paralytic, not having tasted beer for months and not knowing when to stop. This time I poured them into a taxi, but a good time was had by all.

During my stay at Biggin Hill we had a nice surprise when the Windmill Theatre Company came and put on a show in one of the hangars, which was equipped with a stage. The Windmill was famous for never having closed its doors right through the Blitz and for the very comely girls who formed the chorus. Some posed nude on the stage but were forbidden to move until the scene changed and the stage lights were out. Unfortunately, they did not do this at Biggin but with several hundred sex-starved airmen in the audience one supposes that this was too much of a risk. Afterwards the girls were entertained in the officers' mess but were closely chaperoned by some tough ladies. So, apart from exchanging a few words, there was nothing doing in the sex or romance stakes. Some of the many homosexual stagehands who came with them went looking for nice officers to enjoy but had no luck. One who penetrated the Free French officers' quarters was rewarded by being thrown out of an upstairs window but survived the experience.

The Windmill show went round all eleven group sector stations and in due course invited a few officers from each unit to come to the Windmill itself. The place was seething with pilots, every one of whom paid as much attention to avoiding contact with the 'queers' (as they were then called) as they did to getting close to the girls who, however, were as closely chaperoned as before. The Free French contingent got fed up and then left well before the end. They drove off in their vehicle and left their driver high and dry in London with no money. Fortunately the driver knew where our transport was parked and when we finally came out he asked if he could get a lift with us. Of course we had no objection but we thought very poorly of the French for their action.

Later in the war, Biggin Hill destroyed its thousandth enemy aircraft and a big celebration was organised in London to which everyone who had flown at Biggin was supposed to have been invited. No invitation reached me but I was not sorry in the end because the 'bash' cost several hundred pounds more than allowed for, so everyone had to chip in to make up the deficit. The Chief Intelligence Officer at Biggin Hill, who was pretty unscrupulous about making 'probable' kills into 'confirmed' kills, may have accounted for some of the thousand and it was he who organised the party. This was not to detract from Biggin's fine record in any way.

Later in my service at Biggin much 'alarm and despondency' (a term greatly used in the RAF at the time) was caused among the higher ranks by the appearance in our skies of German reconnaissance aircraft flying at 43,000 feet. They were fully pressurized and powered by highly supercharged, two-stroke diesel engines (another example of German mastery of diesel technology). The Allied air forces had nothing that could get anywhere near this height so a special 'High Altitude Unit' was formed, flying stripped-down Spitfire IXHFs with just two machine guns for armament and no armour. Meanwhile, Rolls-Royce worked flat out on a three-speed supercharger. By one means or another a pilot eventually intercepted and shot at a German reconnaissance plane. I don't believe he hit it but we saw no more of them. A single bullet hole would have been enough to cause fatal decompression.

I remember we had some schoolboys on the camp and I had one sitting in the cockpit of a Spitfire. I told him not to touch anything while I told him how the controls worked, whereupon he pressed a button and blew up the IFF (friend or foe indicator) equipment behind the cockpit, causing a loud bang and a cloud of smoke. This button was provided specifically for destroying the IFF to prevent it from falling into enemy hands in the event of landing in France. It would also self-destruct in a violent crash-landing. What I said to the boy I do not remember, but he was scared enough anyway.

A French lady living near Biggin Hill was prepared to serve a horse steak for a moderate price. I had no qualms about eating horsemeat, for the horse is a clean animal and lives on grass just like cows. The meal was pleasant enough but really we were so well fed in the mess there was no reason to go elsewhere except for the experience. There was an officers' dining-in night, which I think was on 1 April 1943, presumably to celebrate the formation of the RAF on 1 April 1918. Unless on leave or ill, attendance was mandatory. Senior officers sat at the top of the table, of course, while the rest of us sat anywhere on the other tables. At the very end sat the most junior officer in the mess, whose job it was to make the royal toast when requested to do so by the Group Captain. After this, the latter said, 'Gentlemen, you may smoke.' Of particular interest was the Free French Squadron who had a barrel of French wine. This suggests that French and English fishing boats were meeting mid-Channel in spite of the Germans.

To close on my service with 611 Squadron, a serious (and extremely costly) incident led to the discovery of jet-streams in the high atmosphere which could blow at 150 mph usually from north-west to south-east. A squadron of Spitfire IXHFs was sent to Predannack, where we had been earlier, to patrol towards the Breton Peninsula. They were above cloud at great height all the time and never saw the ground at all. When the patrol

Artist sketches of 611 pilots. Wing Commander Thomas (centre) with the author on his left and Squadron Leader Armstrong immediately above him

time was over the squadron turned into a reciprocal course to return home. After coming down through the cloud they saw cliffs with an airfield on top as they went into circuit and landed only to find that they were on a *Luftwaffe* base south-east of Brittany. The Germans were no doubt cock-a-hoop over the free gift of twelve of the RAF's latest fighters. They allowed the CO to use a radio to tell his base in England what had happened. The jet-stream had blown the squadron 100 miles south-east of where they thought they were.

While with 611 Squadron at Biggin Hill, I went on twenty-five operational flights including some anti-rhubarb patrols. This was not a high rate of activity overall and it showed even more in my last two months there. My last flight with 611 Squadron took place on 3 April 1943 and this was a humble cannon test. I think it was realised that my tour of operational flying was getting to be too long and I was overdue for a rest. When operational flying units asked for more instructors, I was posted in early May to 57 OTU at Boulmer in Northumberland, to my great regret at the time.

Chapter 11

Instructing at OTU (Operational Training Unit)

By the greatest of good fortune my stay at Boulmer lasted only a few days. It was a dump of a place then and was not improved by the fact that the CO was none other than the savage wing commander from Malta. One period of service under this gentleman was quite enough. In the few days of flying I can remember that the wind never seemed to blow straight down the main runway. Landing a Spitfire in a slight cross-wind was no problem for an experienced pilot but to a beginner it was entirely another matter and undercarriages were being broken, leading to smashed propellers and bent flaps. In desperation the CFI, whose name I have completely forgotten, had straw put on the runway so that a Spitfire's wheels could skid for a few yards on touchdown rather than being snapped off, but to no avail that I can remember.

RAF Boulmer was being shut down and we were posted elsewhere, myself to No. 56 OTU at RAF Tealing just north of Dundee where I stayed from mid-May to Christmas 1943 and had the time of my life. I

A Hurricane Mk. II. Photo courtesy of MAP Sleaford

imagine this was due in part to my old CO from 611 Squadron in Drem, who was now CFI as Wing Commander Watkins and who, I felt, had always regretted being obliged to send me to Malta. I reported to him when I arrived and he told me he wanted me to teach 'dive bombing'. I said I had never dropped a bomb in my life and he said he was well aware of that. He gave me a small flight consisting of two brand-new Hurricanes Mark II and I think three 'Miles Master' two-seat trainers fitted with bomb racks. My job was to teach myself dive-bombing in a Master and then in a Hurricane, following which I would take pupils from the other flights, give them dual instruction in the Master then turn them loose in one of my precious Hurricanes. There was a bombing range on the coastal sands just south of the River Tay estuary which was staffed by a couple of RAF men who plotted the fall of the bombs, then phoned to report results.

Very early in my time at Tealing I was surprised when the squadron leader equipment officer came up to me in the mess and said that he thought that I should have a new battledress, which was no less than the truth, as mine was old and somewhat tatty. I went to see him in his office and he came up with a new battledress, together with shoes and socks, shirts and a new tie. I had never been so generously treated before, and after this he invited me to his home, where his wife cooked an uneatably hot curry, which caused me some embarrassment at only being able to eat a little of it. All the officers were very agreeable and it seemed I could do no wrong. Even on the occasions that I did, nobody said a word. The 'Station Master', as the big white chief was known, was as nice as pie to me, although he did order me very nicely to remove the small silver Maltese cross from my uniform. Personal additions to one's uniform were not permitted.

I had become very proficient at the game of snooker and managed to win some pocket money by beating most of those who challenged me. During a deciding match in the group, an officer was going round selling raffle tickets. He had one left and at first I declined to buy as I was concentrating on the snooker. He persisted and so in the end I gave him the money for it. Much to my delight, I won £25 which, with my wedding date approaching, was very welcome.

It was in 1943 that I married the lady of my choice and after a honeymoon in Edinburgh (where we climbed up 140 steps to street level not realising that our hotel had its own lift down to the platforms, and this after a twelve-hour journey without food or drink), my new wife and I took up residence in the Royal Hotel in Dundee, at 12/6 per day for dinner, bed and breakfast. Every morning I got on the telephone to my chief on the flight and asked him if he could see the top of the hill just north of the airfield. If he said it was clear I had to go to the camp but he often said, 'No, Sir, you can go back to bed.' I needed no encouragement.

Wedding day, 1943

I really do not know what I expected of marriage, except of course the sex, of which neither my wife nor I had any experience. It took a few days to settle in, due to a dysfunction on my part to which over-excitement probably contributed. By the time we moved to the hotel in Dundee, we both experienced a sense of wonder that anything could be so beautiful as our consummated love for each other. No one can know this more than once and it seems to me that some young people today, who expect to be sexually active during their teens, may never know the wonder that we experienced. Unfortunately, someone became aware that I was living out of camp, so our romantic idyll was terminated by order of the boss, but it was good while it lasted. Once again I should have been in serious trouble, but no more was said.

While I was at work at the airfield, my wife walked around Dundee. The people were very friendly but she had great difficulty understanding their accent. She nodded and said yes or no at the appropriate moments and hoped that the locals did not think she was too dim to understand. We heard from an aunt of mine that she had relatives living in Dundee and she gave us their address. They lived up the hill in a well-to-do district and they were very hospitable. Like any other town, the gap in living standards between the working class areas and the 'nob-hill' was very noticeable.

With two fully-armed Hurricanes in my little flight I pleaded to be allowed to do 'readiness', like on squadron, but my pleas went in vain. I did get one operational flight on convoy escort but nothing untoward occurred. The daily routine was humdrum but a nice rest, and there were a few events to liven things up a bit. There was a Fleet Air Arm flying training unit just to the west of Dundee and they asked if they could 'borrow' an experienced instructor to help them. An RAF officer was duly sent but arrived back in disgrace after a few weeks, his error being to have flown under the Tay Bridge. Unfortunately for him, the span he picked to fly under was being painted underneath by two men on a cradle. The wind of the aircraft passage only a few feet below them caused the cradle to swing about violently and the painters lost no time in coming up and telephoning the police. The aircraft was soon identified and the RAF officer was sent packing. He got a rousing reception on his return.

I only had one bad fright during my time at Tealing when I was in the back seat of a 'Master'. The pupil in the front seat misjudged his approach to the 'target' and instead of breaking off he tried to roll the aircraft, which at a few hundred feet is not a good idea. I said 'I've got her' and he immediately let go of the controls, while I corrected the roll just in time and gave him some choice harsh words about being such a bloody idiot.

The general training flights on the airfield flew old Hurricanes Mk. I. These were fitted with the original Merlin I engines in which the coolant was 100 per cent Glycol which in later engines was used at 20 per cent strength as an antifreeze. In any liquid-cooled engine, if white smoke in the exhaust became apparent, it meant a coolant leak which would result in the engine seizing up in a few minutes. (In the Battle of Britain any Me 109 trailing white smoke could be claimed as destroyed because it would never get back across the channel.) In the early Merlin engines with 100 per cent Glycol there was also the serious risk of an engine fire. I was glad we had not been told about this when we trained. One day I was standing outside in the sunshine watching a flight coming into land when the instructor leading it had his engine burst into clouds of white smoke. It was much too low for the pilot to take to his parachute so he very skilfully side-slipped into land (to blow the smoke to one side) on the left side of the runway. There was so much smoke one could only see the propeller and one wing tip; the cockpit was completely obscured. Suddenly the pilot appeared running as fast as he could along the wing, leaning into the slip-stream, then jumping off the wing-tip into the grass. He must have still been doing over 60 mph, and I started running towards his body which was bouncing along the grass. An ambulance soon overtook me going along the perimeter track, but before it reached the pilot he stood up and limped along to meet it. He sprained his ankle – an incredible escape.

On another occasion outside my office I caught the unmistakable sound of an out-of-control aircraft going into a terminal velocity dive. It is a sound like no other. As the aircraft rapidly gains speed the noise increases and when the pitch control on the propeller is overwhelmed the engine revs up to two or three times its normal rate and the howl fills the sky. Then suddenly, silence. I was not near enough to hear or feel the impact. Subsequently, I asked the training flight commander if it was one of his aircraft. He said it was. The pilot was on a routine height climb such as every fighter pilot did. The exercise required the pilot to call control giving his own call sign and say '10,000 feet, oxygen on.' This would be repeated every 5,000 feet up to 25,000 feet.

The dead pilot had not called. So control called him and got an incoherent answer. He sounded as though he was drunk, which is a sure sign of oxygen deprivation. Increasingly urgent calls were made to no effect. The pilot would have passed out at about 18,000 feet and, left to its own devices, the aircraft would begin to tip over and dive, which is what I heard. In this situation, it is quite possible that the pilot came to nearer the ground but would be quite unable to save himself. Not a happy thought.

It had been arranged for an army glider with its 'tug' aircraft to pay a visit to Tealing. The pair arrived and the tug released the glider which made such a precipitous approach that we thought it was going to crash. However, the pilot flared out and landed safely. This very steep approach was to get the glider on the ground very quickly as it would be vulnerable to small arms fire on its approach. The tug and glider were going to give us a demonstration of take-off. This involved the glider in keeping its brakes on while the tug moved forward, stretching the three-inch diameter rubber rope to its maximum extent. At this point the glider pilot let off the brakes that catapulted it forward with a very violent acceleration.

Our CFI said he would like to be on the flight in the glider and we would see him standing in the door between the pilots. I cannot believe that the pilots did not warn him that he would be unable to hang on to the sides of the door when the brakes were released, unless it was a joke that the pilots used to play on senior officers wanting a free trip. At any event, the CFI vanished into the interior of the glider and stood a good chance of smashing into the rear bulkhead and badly injuring himself. I think some kind of soft barrier must have been placed for him to hit without injury. He was shaken but unhurt.

When the officers' mess wanted to have a party somebody remarked that the record collection was worn out. So, for some reason, I was given some money to go and buy some new ones. The more senior officers, of course, wanted old-time waltzes, foxtrots and quick-steps, but what I bought was up-to-date raucous music. One record that I remember was called 'Sorghum Switch'. The seniors in the mess were appalled and sent someone out to buy something more to their liking. I lived under a shadow for a while, but it soon passed.

I had a dose of the flu and was put into the camp hospital for a few days. My colleagues came to visit me with bottles of beer secreted in their battledress tops and I rapidly recovered with the aid of the alcohol. As I was leaving the sick quarters, an instructor whom I did not know very well came out of the MO's room staggering and groaning and went off. I asked the MO, 'What on earth did you do to him, Doc?' He answered, 'He has been posted back onto ops and keeps reporting sick with imaginary complaints to avoid it. So this morning I gave him a large injection in a very tender spot and told him to come back tomorrow for another one. But I don't think he will want one.' The MO was right.

One evening when I was lounging around in the ante-room the phone rang. The mess steward answered it then came in and said 'Flying Officer Smith, please. Group Captain on the phone.' I did not know what to make of it. Group captains are not in the habit of phoning FOs at any time. I went to the phone and said, 'Smith here, Sir,' and he said, 'I want you to go into the mess and pick another five young officers like yourself, and I will send a car to pick you up. I am with the Laird who is throwing a party and we have six young ladies requiring partners.'

Doing as I was told I went back to the ante-room and picked five others. They were agog, thinking about free food and drink, with some aristocratic crumpet thrown in and a ride in the group captain's limo. What more could a young man want? I was not so happy, being just married and not interested in the crumpet, be it ever so aristocratic, and I thought that we were going to have to dance for our supper, or at least perform the strange capering which passes for dancing north of the border. So it proved. There was no food or drink, the young ladies had no doubt been briefed about the randiness of young RAF officers and were not all that friendly. At about 10 p.m. the butler appeared with a decanter of Scotch. We automatically began to slaver like Pavlov's dogs but the Laird said, 'This is much too good for you young men. Giles, give them a bottle of beer.' That was our only reward and there was a marked silence on our return to the camp.

While my new wife and I were in residence at the Royal Hotel in Dundee we saw some surprising sights out of the lounge window which faced the street but at first-floor level. On one occasion an altercation between some men on the other side of the street became a fight and one man was thrown through a shop window. He must have been cut by the flying glass but I cannot remember if he appeared seriously hurt. The most astonishing incident we saw concerned the trams. These came down the slope and either went on to Tay Bridge or turned right up Reform Street. As each tram crossed the points it would stop while the conductor got out and moved the points for the following tram. One evening after a tram had turned right and the conductor moved the points for the Tay Bridge, some youths came out with an iron bar and moved the points to Reform Street again. The next tram came down at some speed, expecting to go straight on, but went screeching round to the right instead. How it did not turn over I do not know, but as a tram cannot be driven backwards it upset the schedule while it was being driven round the block to come back for the Tay Bridge. One imagines the authorities were not amused.

The hotel was joined to the Opera Bar round the corner by a steep flight of stone steps, as the ground sloped steeply down to where the doors to the bar were situated. These steps were presumably for the staff to use but one night a very drunken New Zealander climbed up and came to shake me by the hand, as he was being posted south again. He wrung my hand for a good few minutes then went back to the steep steps, which he fell down from top to bottom. We got up to see if he had hurt himself but heard him chuckle and go back into the bar. Had he not been drunk he probably would have hurt himself badly. He was noted for drinking a pint of beer while hanging by his toes over a roof girder in the mess.

I was having an early drink in the Opera Bar one evening when a Scotsman came in with the 51st Highlander's flash on his uniform. This unit had recently came back from North Africa and had a very high regard for the RAF. The soldier invited me to have a drink but I said I was all right for the time being, whereupon he drew his dirk and stuck it violently in the bar and said, 'You'll have a drink.' Having no wish to upset a fighting man with a dirk, I hastily agreed and then I was there all evening until closing time at 9 pm. Incidentally, ladies were not allowed in bars in Scotland at that time but could sit and have a drink in the hotel lounge. The only other incident in the hotel that I can recall was a Canadian officer who had tried to get a girl up the stairs to a room that he had booked. The hall porter intercepted him and an argument developed. The porter was not to be moved from his guardianship of the moral standing of the hotel and the Canadian eventually gave up.

On a later occasion a group of us were in the dockyard; whether by invitation or because we pushed our way in I cannot remember. At that time small ships were still being built there and the captain of an almost completed ship invited us aboard. We went into his quarters and were astonished to find them most expensively fitted out with mahogany panelling and beautiful furniture. We asked how this came about in wartime and he said that when he came to take the ship over he had found all this lovely gear unclaimed on the dockside and rather than have it go to waste he had it installed for himself. We drank a lot of rum and then invited the captain ashore for beer drinking. He must have had a head as hard as a cannon ball because he outdrank all but one of us. We did not feel well the next day.

In due course the CFI, Wing Commander Watkins, was posted elsewhere and was replaced by Wing Commander Dawson. I am fairly sure that this was his name and my impression of him was that he was of slight build, fair-headed and somewhat effeminate. This latter adjective was the last one that should have been in his description, as was found out when something of his history became known. He had been shot down over France and in his determination to get away had killed some Germans. It was just as well he did get clean away, otherwise he would have been shot. The same would apply if the Germans laid hands on him again during the war and so he was barred from further operations.

Later on in my time at Tealing the flight lieutenant in charge of the Station Flight (whose job it was to fly with instructors and pupils to see that the instructors were doing a good job) came to my dispersal hut and said, 'Right, Smithy, we are going to do some low flying.' With all the ill grace I could muster I said, 'What the hell for?'

He said, 'You practise sneak low-level approach to your bombing range, so I want to see whether you are good at it.' He was senior to me so off we went, with me in front and him lower down in the back. We flew north then he said to me, 'Go down to 200 feet.' I did this without bothering to keep my bearings. When he said, 'Where are we now?' I replied I hadn't the faintest idea. He said, 'Go back and start again.' By this time I was fuming as much with myself as with him, so I went down to fifty feet, lifting over trees (this gives a very sick-making feeling to the man in the back seat because he cannot see it coming). I went between some trees on one wing-tip, eventually pulling up in plenty of time when the hill north of Tealing came in sight (one cannot fly a training aircraft up the side of a hill: there is not enough power) but clearing the top by only twenty feet. Having a good look round to see that there were no other aircraft in the vicinity, I tore down the other side of the hill, pulled a really tight turn to follow the perimeter track, flew between the back of the control tower and the hangar, shut the throttle and pulled up into a stall turn. As the aircraft tipped back the way we had come, I put down the wheels and flaps and plonked it down a few yards down the runway, thus being able to turn off at the first intersection. I taxied back to my dispersal, switched off and after a minute or two I said, 'All right Kenneth?' There was no answer so I turned round and saw him hanging onto the wing as white as a sheet and sweating nonetheless. He picked up his parachute and staggered off. He never spoke to me again. No sense of humour evidently.

There was no doubt that this was a dangerous display and I expected to be summoned by the wing commander to explain myself. Nothing like that took place. A few days later he came round and said, 'You are a bit cramped here, Smithy. Would you like to move to the empty dispersal over there?' I said I would indeed, so some lorries took our gear over. I borrowed some pilots to taxi the aircraft and we set up in our new home. The Squadron Leader Equipment Officer sent six armchairs and a carpet so it was more like the RAC than an RAF dispersal hut. As I said to start with, I had the time of my life.

At some stage during my service at Tealing, the Station Adjutant rang up and instructed me to report to the group captain. I did this and he introduced me to a wing commander who was the OC Training in the group. He then said that he wanted me to fly the wing commander back to his base in Lancashire. I was to get a Met report and prepare to travel shortly.

I saluted and went to get a Met report that said it was hazy towards the west. This proved to be an understatement. Flying above the haze into the sun made the ground invisible. Only by looking back down-sun could the ground be seen at all. I could not find the wing commander's base and began to run short of fuel. I told him that I was going to have to do a forced landing. He had no option but to agree. There did not seem to be a field large enough to land on the wheels and so I did a belly landing without injury, but of course the plywood aircraft suffered badly. The wing commander got the hump big-time, but had to give me a lift to his HQ in the car he had phoned for at the local farm so that I could get a rail warrant back to Tealing. A wearisome cross-country journey.

Arriving back at Dundee station, I had the usual long wait, still carrying my parachute, which is a very awkward thing to handle without a proper bag. Even if a hundred people got off the train, there was only ever a single ticket collector at the top of the long flight of stairs who examined every ticket with care. Once out of the station, I phoned for transport and was duly collected.

Subsequently, two officers were allocated to the job of a board of enquiry into the crash. They interviewed me and asked why I had not put the petrol/air mixture lever to weak for the trip. I replied that for two years on operational aircraft there had not been a mixture lever because it was done automatically and I had not even thought about using it in the Master

A Miles Master trainer. Photo courtesy of MAP Sleaford

aircraft. They understood this and had the grace to admit that, in the pea-soup haze, even the extra half-hour flight using weak mixture probably would not have saved the crash. I heard no more about it.

At Christmas I was posted to 197 Squadron to fly Typhoons at Tangmere.

Chapter 12

Operations on Typhoons

I duly turned up at Tangmere, where nobody was expecting me. This caused me no surprise as the massive organisation which could keep track of hundreds of thousands of individuals never seemed to be able to send a copy of the posting signal to the unit at the receiving end until after the person who had been posted had arrived.

Tangmere was a large and famous fighter airfield on very flat ground, unlike Biggin Hill which was perched on top of an escarpment. Tangmere had a wing-sized satellite (for three squadrons) at Westhampnett a few miles away where I had served in the autumn of 1941. The first noticeable thing was that instead of batmen to serve the officers there were batwomen. Every single man allocated to serve as batman hated the job. This was partly due to the fact that the very idea of service was anathema to the British working man, and partly because as batmen they were treated with a complete lack of consideration by the officers they were obliged to serve (for junior officers there was one batman among five or six). For batwomen the situation could not have been more different. Making beds and looking after men was entirely natural to them, and the buxom wench serving us did so with enthusiasm and in more ways than one. I believe her name was Ivy and she was often available for more intimate services outside working hours, something for which pilots from overseas were very grateful. More of this lady later.

The first thing I saw in dispersal was a large poster of a photograph taken from ground level looking up the skirt of an actress of the day, who was being swung round in a dance with her feet off the floor and her legs wide apart. She was not wearing any knickers so her bare vulva appeared right in the middle of the poster. How this picture ever got out I cannot imagine but it was the squadron's pride and joy. There were young service women in and out of dispersal all day and any one of them could have gone to a female officer to complain, in which case the officer would have come to have a look and demand its removal. However, this did not happen. The young women of the day did not apparently feel the picture degraded their sex and left it at that – a very different view from that held today. Eventually a New Zealand squadron, which flew in to stay the night on their way to somewhere else, broke into our dispersal hut and stole the picture and we never saw it again.

Before moving on to write about operations on Typhoons I think something should be written about the aircraft itself. To this day Spitfires and Hurricanes are taken to epitomise the fighting spirit and glamour of fighter pilots and Typhoons are all but forgotten (but not by the Germans who fought tooth and nail against this name being given to the Euro-fighter because their military had vivid memories of the damage caused by Typhoons out of all proportion to the number of aircraft involved). This name, however, was eventually given to this splendid new aircraft, the need for which will largely have passed before it even reaches squadron service.

The Typhoon was large compared to earlier fighters, weighing seven and a half tons against the Spitfire at three and a half tons. The Sabre engine was like two boxer-type (i.e. horizontally opposed) cylinders of six-a-side, one being placed on top of the other to give twenty-four cylinders with a capacity of thirty-six litres and an output of about 2,100 hp. It was sleeve-valved and early problems were evident in lubricating the sleeves, leading to frequent failure. Eventually the Bristol Aircraft Co. which made sleeve-valved radial engines were obliged to part with their 'nitriding' process to the sleeves to the Napier Engine Co. (makers of the Sabre) which overcame the lubrication problem, but the engine was still tricky to operate, and in particular could not be run at low revs to give fuel economy. Max revs at take-off were 3,600 rpm and lowest safe revs was 2,600 rpm. There was a stop fitted to the 'pitch' lever to prevent a pilot from going below this figure. The engine was very 'fat' so that forward view down the side of it was limited at take-off, and it emitted so much carbon monoxide which leaked into the cockpit that oxygen was always used even at low altitude. (I took one up for an air-test on one occasion and found that when I switched on the oxygen there wasn't any. By this time I was airborne and had to whirl around the airfield desperately trying to stay conscious to get down again).

Starting the Sabre engine was quite a performance. For the first start-up in the day the propeller had to be pushed round by hand to avoid what was called 'hydraulicing', that is oil having dripped into the lower cylinder head which, being incompressible, would result in severe damage to the pistons or cylinder heads or both. This having been done, an airman had to stand just in front of the propeller with a fire extinguisher. The 'Koffman' starter operated by firing a cartridge into a mechanism which turned the engine over and, in the event of the engine not firing, a cascade of burning fuel was liable to run down into the air-intake which had to be extinguished before another cartridge was fired. (There were five cartridges on one load).

The radiator was situated right under the engine with the air-intake in the middle of it. It was the worst possible place to put the radiator for an aircraft engaged in ground attacks but the Typhoon was designed as a very fast fighter (it was the first one able to exceed 400 mph in level flight) and its performance comfortably exceeded that of the Focke Wolf 190 at least up to 20,000 feet. This radiator situated where it was made it impossible to survive 'ditching' the aircraft other than in very shallow water because, when it hit the water, the aircraft flipped over on its back and, with its huge engine, sank so quickly that the pilot could not force his way out against the flow of water. He drowned where he sat in the cockpit. Only one pilot was known to have survived ditching in deep water. He did this by getting half out of the cockpit while steering the aircraft with one hand inside. When the aircraft hit the water and tipped up on its nose, the pilot was flung out like a stone from a catapult. He was soon picked up. He had broken one leg, but it was a hell of a lot better than being drowned.

The Typhoon airframe also had a bad start in life. Several aircraft apparently dived vertically into the ground without the pilot getting a word out over his radio. The answer to this came from a pilot (who must have had the reactions of a cat) who, hearing an unpleasant noise behind him, was out of his cockpit in seconds and as he fell away he saw the whole tail assembly of his Typhoon break off from the fuselage and then be towed vertically downwards by the four control cables attached to the elevators and rudder. The very sudden negative 'g' caused by the instantaneous change from the horizontal to the vertical would have caused the pilot to crack his skull on the cockpit canopy and knock himself out, hence no word from him. To strengthen the tail about a dozen or so straps of metal were rivetted around the point where the tail assembly joined the fuselage and this problem was eliminated.

By the time I started to fly Typhoons the early design of a hump-backed fuselage, with a car-type door (complete with wind-down windows) on each side and a very poor view to the rear, had given way to the series 1B, which had a 'bubble' hood giving a perfect all-round view. This had a winder so one could open or close it with the minimum of effort. It could also, of course, be jettisoned. My first flight was on 31 December following which I undertook a series of training flights. I had no difficulty with the Typhoon.

197 Squadron together with 257 (Burma) Squadron and I think 266 (Rhodesia) Squadron formed 146 Wing in 84 Group of the 2nd Tactical Air Force. I believe there were two other squadrons in the wing, but I do not think we ever came into contact with them as they were based elsewhere. The five-squadron wing was under the command of the fearsome Group Captain 'Kill-em' Gillam. Nothing would stop him from attacking the target of the day. If there was heavy cloud cover (which previously no one had attempted to fly through with the clumsy Typhoon), he would lead the first squadron up through the cloud and then call the

A Typhoon 1B in flight. Photo courtesy of MAP Sleaford

other squadrons up one at a time until they were all in formation. After dead-reckoning the way to the target, he would leave the squadrons orbiting while he alone went down through the cloud to find the target. He would then fly around and around it, totally ignoring the flak, calling the squadrons down. When he saw them break cloud, he would direct them to the target. How he survived is a mystery. In fact he continued to attack the enemy with only a number two for company right to the end of he war in Europe, after which I believe he returned, much decorated, to his family business.

The business of air-to-ground attack formed a stark contrast to that of air fighting. The latter called for great skill and courage to be effective and hopefully to survive. Formation leaders tended to survive the longest. Having survived long enough to become leaders, their experience gave them the edge and if formation was attacked it would be from the rear and the leader would be flying in front. However, ground attack depended not so much on flying skills but on the courage to attack no matter how much flak the enemy put up, and it was formation leaders who tended to get shot down first.

The wing was equipped with bomb racks or long-range drop-tanks. Our task was to 'blind' the Germans by taking out their radar stations and also to destroy the 'ski' sites from which the V1 pilotless flying bombs were launched against London. The Germans were able to re-erect or build new ones over night and so we had to keep at it to keep the ski sites to a minimum. Enemy radar sites were easily seen being placed near the coast but, while finding them was easy, attacking them was anything but, as they were heavily defended with light calibre flak through which our aircraft were obliged to fly in a steep dive to drop our bombs. I did not notice the flak so much in the dive itself because all my attention was on the target, but on the run-in and when pulling out of the dive the flak was so intense I wondered how it could miss. The 'tracer' rounds seem to climb ever so slowly then rush past at tremendous speed, a very alarming feeling. Of course, they did not always miss and claimed a number of aircraft shot down or badly damaged.

My first operational flight was on 14 January when we attacked Target No. 107 and my remarks are 'bombing very good, no flak'. On the same day we attacked Target No. 41 when my aircraft was holed in six places. On 25 January we had an uneventful trip with cloud obscuring whatever we were looking for.

On another occasion a lump of shrapnel came in the side of my cockpit and took out my engine instruments (coolant temperature and oil pressure) so I would have no warning of impending engine failure. As a Typhoon could not be ditched, I climbed up to 8,000 feet on my own to give me plenty of time to call 'mayday' before bailing out. Fortunately nothing happened but I had a miserable trip back with a freezing draught blowing through the shrapnel hole and hot oil dripping down my right leg.

One dive-bombing attack which put the Germans in fear of Typhoons resulted from one aircraft receiving a direct hit and, in spite of the aircraft starting to come apart, the pilot (evidently realising he was not going to survive) let his bombs go and then dived his plane straight into the radar unit. Seven and a half tons of Typhoon arriving at over 450 mph completely destroyed the unit and the German staff (who were captured soon after the second front opened) apparently lost no time in letting it be known that Typhoon pilots were prepared to copy the Japanese suicide bombers if the occasion demanded it. This, of course, was not true, but it did us no harm at all if the Germans chose to believe it.

After the trip on 21 January I went on leave for a week and my wife and I had found out which pub received its beer ration on which day, so we were never short of a drink. We had a wonderful week but I began to feel queer in the train going back and so I reported sick when back at Tangmere. The MO pulled down the lower lids of my eyes and said, 'We send you on leave to keep fit, not to have so much sex that you can hardly stand.' I replied that I kept fit in camp and wanted to enjoy myself at home. He prescribed forty-eight hours of bed-rest. I felt a bit of a fool over this but had the pleasure of Ivy clucking over me and fetching my food. I think she knew full well what was the matter with me.

Operations continued with an attack on 14 February on which I remarked in my logbook 'Little heavy and some light flak' and on 18 February we did a co-operative exercise with tank landing craft on which I remarked 'Damn good beat up.' On 24 February an attack was made on Target No. 72 and I wrote 'Squadron bombing very good.' There were two more trips in February, both of which were obscured by cloud and I remarked, 'Waste of time.'

I wrote earlier about our buxom batwoman often being available for more intimate services. One evening a number of us were drinking in a pub in Chichester when one remarked 'God, I could do with Ivy tonight.' Another said, 'So could I', whereupon both dashed outside, stole the first bicycles they found and tried to race each other to be the first to claim Ivy. In half an hour or so they were back, having put the bicycles back were they found them. Apparently it was the wrong time of the month for Ivy, something neither of them had thought about.

Apparently no plans for further use of Typhoons had been made, owing to the conviction in the upper echelons of the RAF that while fighter pilots were wonderful for defence and escorting bombers, left to their own devices they were incapable of finding and attacking small targets in France.

However, someone persuaded the top brass to give us a test and our squadron was given the task of finding and destroying a tiny brick-built bridge on a French farm (I believe other squadrons were given similar tasks). We did find it and we did destroy it and I can imagine its owner, watching from a distance as his little bridge was reduced to its component bricks by twelve powerful aircraft, thinking 'Ah, les Anglais, ils sont fous.'

Early in March I did a couple of night flying trips. With the restricted vision down the side of the engine, keeping straight until the tail came up was a bit of a problem. If the flare-path lights appeared to be moving to the right, it meant the aircraft was swinging left, and vice versa. Likewise on landing. While on one of these trips I saw the exhaust flares of another Typhoon. I flew up closer to him and could see that he had his 'head in his office' showing he was flying on instruments, although it was a clear night with a good horizon. I flew into close formation and the pilot still did not see me. So, very unkindly, I put on my navigation lights and he suddenly had a bright red light only about ten feet away on his right. He shied away to the left like a frightened horse and I switched off my lights. The pilot did not report the incident, luckily for me.

The inland targets we began to attack were railways, marshalling yards and bridges, to disrupt the German transport plans and other places simply identified by a 'target number' (but I have long forgotten what these were). Opposition (flak) varied greatly, some being very fierce, some less so. Examples of this will appear later.

On 10 March 1944 the Squadron moved to Manston in the Isle of Thanet to replace 609 Squadron for a while. 609 under the leadership of Squadron Leader Beamont (later chief test pilot for English Electric and the only man ever to fly the TSR2 bomber which was abandoned by the British Government) had been flying with extra-long range tanks right down to the German border. They encountered many *Luftwaffe* training squadrons, when their practice was to fly straight through and and shoot the leader down then pick off the trainees who scattered in panic. The situation became so bad for the Germans, I believe, that they issued orders that all aircraft were to land if within a hundred kilometres of 609, once it had been identified.

In the move to Manston, the CO and regular pilots flew the aircraft while, as supernumerary flight lieutenant, I was given the job of getting the rest of the pilots to Manston by road. An RAF bus was provided with a driver. The furnishings of the bus were pretty sparse, but it was a lot more comfortable than being driven in a truck. We were driving through a small picturesque town in Kent when I stopped the driver for everyone to have tea and hopefully some buns at a substantial looking café. There were about a dozen of us and we trooped in to occupy three tables and I think that some of those present shifted around to make room for us. One of us was a gifted player of the clarinet, which he had with him. Another had been a drummer and, while there were obviously no drums, he used empty bottles on the back of a tea tray to beat out a good rhythm to accompany the clarinet. It was really quite a good show and the locals thoroughly enjoyed it. After thirty minutes or so, I called time and, as we went out, the locals thanked us and wished us well. We then drove on to Manston.

On our short stay at Manston two of our pilots attempted to emulate what 609 had been doing. The only result of this effort was that the leader of the pair hit an aerial mast and lost about three feet off one wing-tip. The aircraft would not keep level below about 200 mph so the pilot had the choice of belly-landing at too high a speed or landing on his wheels, hoping he could keep straight and stop before hitting the boundary. He chose the latter but unfortunately hit a bump so the undamaged wing lifted and the pilot found himself heading for a hangar. He had to pull his wheels up and while he himself was unhurt he was severely shaken.

We also witnessed a USAF B17 belly landing (after being shot-up) on the grass emergency strip built especially for crippled aircraft to land on. Our squadron van went over and found that the only occupant was the pilot, and when he was asked what happened to his crew he said that they didn't think the aircraft would make it back to the UK and, rather than risk drowning if it ditched, they elected to jump out over France and become POWs. The pilot didn't seem to think that this was very odd but we did. Nobody jumped from an RAF bomber unless ordered to do so.

On 1 April 1944 I flew with alcohol in me for the first and last time. We were billeted in a disgusting old hotel at Westgate which was absolutely infested with cockroaches and steam bugs. It poured with rain all one day and the Met Office said it would pour all next day as well. After dinner four of us each bought a crate of beer and retired to a room to play cards till 3 a.m. when we ran out of beer and went to bed very drunk. Unfortunately, it stopped raining and at 6 a.m. the batman woke me to say I was required down at the airfield. We stopped en route to pick up a NCO pilot (who was cold sober) and on arrival at our squadron hut were sent on a weather recce.

I was leading and I set the wrong course for the wrong length of time so, when we pulled up to cross the French coast, we found ourselves flying over Calais harbour at only 2,000 feet. I have never seen so much flak in my life and my unfortunate No. 2 and I weaved about frantically, climbing at full throttle, and somehow got through this super-hot reception. It sobered me up more than somewhat and when we returned safely my No. 2 had some pithy remarks to make in spite of the difference in rank. I didn't blame him. I have forgotten the NCO's real name but his nickname was

Pork-Sword, an obscure reference to his magical ability to get himself laid at short notice wherever he was. He did not seem to be any better endowed than the rest of us so the reason for his success in this endeavour remained a mystery.

While at Manston we went to visit the Navy small boats station at Margate. As we drove up we witnessed a group of three MGBs (motor gun boats) preparing for their sortie that night. In command of this lot was a Scotsman with a fiery red beard and, although he was only 5′6″ or so, he looked fearsome in the extreme.

As a point of interest, these MGBs had three marine-type Merlin engines, the centre one being placed further forward that the others. In the tiny space between the two side engines and the deck crouched an engineer who had to wear ear plugs. His commands came through a repeater dial from the bridge, as was usual at the time. The fuel was high octane petrol which made these boats prone to explosion if hit by gunfire, unlike the German equivalent, called E-boats, which were diesel-powered. The boats could reach over forty knots. Armament was a 40 mm cannon on the front and rear and a number of machine guns. Grappling hooks were at the ready down the sides. It was their practice, apparently, to approach small German coastal vessels very quietly, then, with a blast of power, come alongside, fling over their grappling hooks and swarm aboard to kill the crew and plant explosives charges in the bilges. What a terrifying outfit.

We had a trip around the Thames estuary flak platforms in an MTB (T for torpedo) powered by three Napier Lion engines. This was to bring mail to the men who staffed these platforms and to take their letters back. It was a pleasant trip except for the fear that we might be called upon for an offensive sortie. Nothing untoward occurred and our CO was allowed to bring the boat back into harbour which he did like an expert.

At the end of March the squadron moved back to Tangmere. I do not remember going back on the bus and so perhaps I flew and somebody else did the run by bus. On 2 April we flew to Thorney Island and then back to Tangmere, but in the brief stop-over at Thorney I took an aircraft up on air-test and found that the air-speed indicator was not working. This was tricky. A Spitfire gives a long warning of a dangerous stall by pronounced shuddering. A Typhoon does not. It stalls and falls sharply. I survived two flights before the air-speed indicator was made to work and this was by reason of landing much faster than usual, but it gave me a couple of bad frights.

I think it was just after we came back from Thorney Island that in the ante-room of the officers' mess (actually it was really the lounge so why it was called the ante-room I have no idea) there appeared a pair of sooty foot-prints up the wall, across the ceiling and down the opposite wall. This does not sound much, but the ceilings must have been twelve feet high and so some sort of construction must have been put up and then moved several times to get from one side of the room to the other.

We thought we should do something to decorate the ceiling and someone put forward the idea of putting a 'bottom' print right in the middle, so one night when the mess was quiet and the female officers had gone (which they were obliged to at 10 p.m.) we erected three heavy tables from the dining room, one on top of the other, and built a ramp out of the indestructible mess chairs. Conveniently an officer of slight build had drunk himself unconscious so we took down his trousers, wetted his bottom with beer and smeared it with soot from the chimney. He was then handed up by some of the stronger members to others on top of the stack of tables, who lifted him by his waist and bumped his bottom on the ceiling. Viewing the results we decided there was no mistaking what it was, but I often wonder what the victim thought when he found his underpants full of soot next morning.

A very handsome and dashing public schoolboy was posted to us. He was completely reckless and a bloody menace to anyone flying with him. A very experienced NCO pilot took me aside one day and said, 'Smithy, if I have to fly No. 2 to that bastard again I am going to shoot him down myself.' (We did not observe differences in rank in private.) I said, 'We have not had this conversation but if you do shoot him down make sure you make a good job of it.'

Subsequently the officer was shot down in France, became a POW and was involved in a mass prisoner-of-war breakout where the Gestapo shot them. None of us shed a tear for him, but some local people who had come to know him thought he epitomised the fighter-type. Little did they know.

Our oxygen masks started to be made of synthetic rubber, although we did not realise this until two pilots suddenly proved to be allergic to this material and their faces came out in dreadful sores, keeping them grounded for some time. It meant that they had to wear natural rubber masks, which were still available.

On 3 April 1944 my old flight commander from 154 Squadron who had become Squadron Leader 'Ronnie' Fokes invited me to become flight commander of 'B' flight on his 257 (Burma) Squadron. I accepted with alacrity, as my rank was already flight lieutenant and as such I was only supernumery on 197 Squadron. Serving under Ronnie was a pleasure. He never raised his voice but his command was absolute and he was very experienced, having served on Typhoon squadrons since the aircraft came into service. I cannot remember the proper name of my opposite number on 'A' flight, but his nickname was 'Barney'. On each flight there were (as far as I remember) twelve pilots and I was very careful to share out operations amongst them so no one had to fly too many successive sorties.

My most senior flight member was my deputy so I could also leave myself off, rather than running myself into nervous exhaustion. When the CO did not make a trip, either Barney or myself would lead, although this would be with two instead of three sections of four.

There were only two operations while 257 remained at Tangmere and one was a weather recce in the Cap de la Hague region. The other was a hunt for targets when we split into pairs looking for transport to shoot up or whatever we could find. My logbook says 'Found empty goods train; very satisfactory shoot up.' Unhappily an experienced pilot failed to return.

Then 257 Squadron, along with 197 Squadron and 266 (Rhodesia) Squadron moved to a wire-mesh airfield on the western shore of the Solent. There were just two steel mesh runways, one of which ran almost into the water, and a signals section, parachute store, mess tents and working facilities had all been put into place before we arrived. Also provided near each of the three dispersal areas was a twenty-foot deep pit into which delayed action bombs which had 'hung-up' and been brought back were tipped to explode at their leisure. On one occasion I helped with three others to carry a bomb to our pit and my 125 pound share of the load took just about all my strength.

The next ten days or so were spent on exercises of one sort or another. On one of these we were supposed to fly to Llanbedr in Wales, but the cloud was sitting on the hill tops so we were diverted and landed at Fairwood Common. The weather obliged us to stay the night and apart from being refuelled there were no servicing facilities for Typhoons. So next morning we had to do our own basic checks after which we flew back to base (on the map this is shown as 'Needs Oar Point').

During this period the whole wing, totalling thirty-six aircraft, took off one cloudy day on an exercise to practise getting a large number of aircraft up through cloud without hitting one another or getting widely separated, thus using precious fuel getting together again. My squadron 257 had just come out above the cloud, 197 was still in it while 266 was still below it. Very suddenly the ground controller called out that there was a 'bandit' over the Isle Of Wight and this unlucky German broke cloud right in front of 266 and was promptly shot down, crashing not far from our airfield and without bursting into flames. Once the excitement died down we got on with the exercise, landing about an hour later and after de-briefing and a meal we went into our tents for a rest, only to find a heap of completely smashed German bodies piled up in the middle of the field. This gruesome sight did not bother us a lot and after an operation in the afternoon, when we experienced very heavy accurate flak, the bodies had gone when we got back and so we thought no more about it.

However, a couple of months later some civilian intelligence men arrived on the airfield to tell us the story of what resulted from the German aircraft

Pilots of 257 (Burma) Squadron. CO is standing against the propeller, with the author on his right. Photo courtesy of Grub Street in Typhoon Attack

being shot down. The thought at first was that it had come for a sneak preview of our invasion preparations and had just been unlucky. An examination of the bodies, however, showed there were two more in the aircraft than usual, that these bodies were wearing ground staff uniform and none of the crew had followed the rigid rule in the *Luftwaffe* and in the RAF of emptying one's pockets of all personal items before going on operations. In any case ground crew would not have been carried over enemy territory, if for no other reason than the very cramped space. One item found was a brothel ticket with an address on it so it was known that the aircraft had set out from central France, but gave no guide as to why it was over the Isle of Wight.

As it happened an officer from the same German squadron was a POW and he was brought out from the prison camp and taken out to dinner by intelligence men who told him that one of his colleagues had flown over with the ground crew to surrender, but we did not know what they wanted and so they were shot down. The German POW was furious at the idea that any of his squadron would surrender and said so. The subject was dropped for a while and more wine was drunk, then it was brought up again. The German, who had not had a drink for months, eventually said he and others had flown from France to a base in Holland with their ground crews prior to a raid that night on London. It was during this raid that he was shot down.

They said thanks very much and bundled the POW back to camp. The Air Ministry was contacted and told to expect a raid from the Dutch airfield. In response to this several night-fighter Mosquitoes were despatched to Holland and one by one they shot down the first six bombers into the sea. The German controller realised that something was very much amiss and aborted the operation, so London was saved from more death and destruction. Why a German pilot flew north to IOW instead of north-east Holland remained a mystery.

A problem we had on this landing ground was caused by the Navy, who had a large flotilla of landing craft anchored in the Solent, each one flying a balloon as a deterrent against low-level aircraft attack. This did not worry us at all in fine weather but when it was cloudy the Navy did not pull their balloons down low enough for us to fly the down-wind leg of our landing approach safely over all the boats. Our wing commander complained to HQ but if the complaints ever reached the Navy Commander he took no notice. Quite by accident we got our own back when one of our inexperienced pilots, who was with us in an attack near Cherbourg, turned the wrong way as he pulled out of his dive (something an experienced pilot would never do) and, noticing his absence, our leader called something like 'Blue 4, Red 1, where are you?' The answer came 'Red 1, Blue 4, I took a wrong turning but am coming back.' He was in no danger so we all flew home with Blue 4 a few minutes behind, blissfully unaware that one of his bombs had 'hung-up'.

We had just landed when he came into his down-wind leg which is when his bomb chose to fall off. As he had not turned off his fusing switches it exploded on impact right alongside the naval commander's barge, which rocked so violently it took several tons of sea-water aboard, all but drowning the crew. The next thing was the arrival on our beach of the Naval Commander in a rubber dinghy. He stormed up to our airfield and bellowed, 'You did that on purpose, you bastard' at our wing commander. The two of them went into the wing commander's caravan where the Navy's voice continued to shout. After a few minutes the Navy stormed out again. Our wing commander, I believe, told the Navy that if he didn't pull his balloons lower in cloudy weather he wouldn't miss next time. We were all highly amused by this.

After the incident of the solitary 'bandit' over the Isle of Wight, the next day we attacked target No. 60, and my notes say, 'Flak accurate, bombing fair, landed at Tangmere.' A few days passed during which we flew to Thorney Island and back again. I presume that whatever we went there for was cancelled.

Trouble broke out with the ground crews who were fed up with always having to eat unpeeled potatoes. There were nothing like enough cook-house staff to peel potatoes for everyone and so it was decided that each airman had to peel a potato before sitting down for his meal. These would be cooked for the second shift of airmen, then theirs for the third who would do the same for the first shift the next day. The airmen were furious that there were never any peeled potatoes at the end of it. It transpired that the sergeant cook had been 'persuaded' by his fellow NCOs to give them all the cooked and peeled potatoes for their own consumption.

On 23 April we all flew to Manston, and while the aircraft were refuelled and bombs put on, we went to a briefing for an attack on railway sheds at Mons. At the end of the briefing the 'spy' put on the map the latest information about 'flak' positions in the area which was very dense indeed. I got that awful feeling in the gut when I knew it was going to be a bad one and said, 'Oh Jesus' to myself, then glanced around to make sure I hadn't said it out loud. Afterwards we went to where our aircraft were standing and all the pilots had the usual 'nervous pee' on the grass. If there was any delay most would have to go again. Once 'press tits' time came and you were on your way, it was not quite so bad until you got there.

My logbook oddly enough says, 'Very good show, bombing excellent, flak going out' so I had worked myself into a bad fright for which in the end there was no need. No doubt others felt the same. As we took off we could see fleets of B17s coming back from Germany, accompanied by their escort fighters. They evidently saw us, as one of them had the cheek to 'bounce' one of our formation flying on the extreme right-hand side. Being on the same side and therefore looking across to the left, I did not see the attack. At the debriefing meeting the pilot told the wing commander that he had been shot at by a P47 Thunderbolt (a big radial-engined brute of an aircraft that weighed over eight tons). He had not been hit but, as the P47 went past, the pilot had fired at it. The wing commander said, 'Did it go down?' and the pilot said, 'No, Sir.'

'Well, that's no bloody good, is it? When you shoot at something, for Christ sake make sure you hit it.'

As we landed one and a half hours later, the US bomber stream was still coming back and we wondered how many aircraft were involved. It must have been a massive attack.

That afternoon we went again to target No. 74, where I record 'Bombing fair, no flak.' Two days later we went to attack a railway station at Folligny, but we were recalled and dropped our bombs in the sea. That afternoon we attacked a bridge near Cherbourg against which I recorded, 'Bombing good, little flak.' The next day we flew to Thorney Island again, where we were addressed by General Eisenhower who was the C.-in-C. of operation 'Overlord', or the invasion of the Continent. He was a short man and had to stand on a box. He welcomed us as the 'Allied Team', which we thought was a cheek as we had been at it long before he arrived. He said he wished he could come with us on our operation that day, to which one wag said, 'You can have my place, mate,' but I don't think he heard.

We went off to attack target No. 115 to which I wrote, 'Bombing very good, heavy flak also good.' Thereafter there was a few days' gap when I probably went on leave, but on 3 May we bombed target No. 59, to which I added, 'Bombing excellent, little light flak.' On 5 May we went again to Manston from where we attacked marshalling yards at Hazebrouck, with remarks 'Bombing excellent, some light flak, squadron flying wizard.' We came back from Manston only to go again on 7 May when we bombed sidings at Dunkerque against which I make no remarks, then in the afternoon bombed the marshalling yards at Arras. Cloud obscured the target but we found two factories to attack. There was no flak.

We were frequently able to leave camp after operations for the day had finished and on most occasions we went to our favourite watering hole which was The Rose and Crown at Brockenhurst, where large quantities of beer were dispatched. All our names were written on the bar ceiling. Mine said 'Flight Lieutenant Smith, going down now, Sir', a reference to the comic radio show *I.T.M.A.*, which did so much to maintain civilian morale in the war. The names stayed there for years after the war but were eventually painted out when interest in them was lost.

On 8 May we flew to Tangmere, from where we attacked marshalling yards at Bethune, against which I remark 'Wizard prang, flak over coast going in, inaccurate.' That afternoon we attacked target No. 109, which I recorded with the remarks 'Bombing fair, little light flak, led squadron.' On 9 May we attacked marshalling yards at Rouen 'bombing perfect, flak accurate and dense'. On 11 May we set out to bomb the radar at Cap d'Antifer where I did not drop bombs but escorted my No. 2 home for some reason. On 12 May we flew to Tangmere again from where we attacked a bridge at Hornoy which proved difficult to find and got no direct hits; on the same day we had a go at the radar site at St Aubin – 'Target not located, bombed unidentified structure.' We did this again on 15 May, and this time 'Bombing and shooting good, target probably written off, no flak.'

One day when the operation was stood down, the CO Ronnie Fokes said to me, 'Grab yourself a towel, Smithy, and we will fly to Tangmere for a bath.' We flew off, parked our two aircraft near the watch office and went for a luxurious bath, using soap that we pinched from somebody's room. Normally keeping bodily clean meant sqatting in a large canvas bucket in the field outside the tent. There were no women around so this was no problem, but it could be chilly.

This intense activity continued. But it was about this time that some bright spark in the War Office said we should drop smoke on the Germans as our troops went ashore. Of all the asinine ideas (one of Churchill's?)! The author must have thought smoke stops where you lay it. In fact, of course, the wind blows it away, and the slightest breeze from the prevailing SW direction would have blown it over our troops and blinded them. I had visions of two old generals sitting over their *chota peg* in their club, one saying to the other, 'Great stuff smoke, old boy; used it against the Pathans in '33.'

Our wing was given the job because we were still fitted with the bomb-racks necessary to carry the smoke canisters, while Typhoons in general had been fitted with rocket-racks (eight rockets fired in pairs, a deadly weapon). I went to the briefing for using smoke, and learned that it involved flying straight and level at fifty feet over 250,000 Germans with their incredible anti-aircraft fire power and I did not think that any aircraft would get 500 yards without being shot to pieces, let alone five miles. Each squadron had to provide a first team of two with a reserve of another two and when my name came out of the hat to lead 257's first team I just stood there and felt physically sick.

This led to my very worst period in the RAF. The dread of what was to come was with me every waking moment. I had put my life on the line of my own volition, rescuing a Spitfire from a delayed-action bomb in Malta, but now I was expected (with others) to commit suicide for no good purpose at all. I couldn't run away, I couldn't cry on anyone's shoulder or tell them how I felt, I was a flight commander with pilots to lead and couldn't give any sign that anything was amiss, if I wanted to keep their respect and trust.

We practised laying smoke over much of Hampshire and had the only amusing incident during that time when the CO of 197 Squadron accidentally pressed the smoke button while taxiing out for practice and he and his aircraft disappeared in a cloud of very thick white smoke. He did what he thought was the right thing, stopped his aircraft and got out, but as soon as he let go of it he could not see it any more and he couldn't even see his own feet. He tried to walk out of the smoke which was spreading but, having no point of reference, walked in circles. We could hear loud coughing and a prize selection of four-letter words but it was several minutes before he appeared, red-faced and choking. We all cheered him, laughing at the same time but he stomped off. He was a bully and an unpleasant man, but to give him his due he would not let his pilots draw lots to lead the smoke team but insisted he would do it himself.

I do not know how I got through the two to three weeks before the smoke idea was abandoned. As time went by I became more and more desperate, trying to hold myself together and in the end I suppose it was the now derided 'stiff upper lip' which kept me going. Once the idea was dropped I forgot about it, but my nervous system did not forget about it and I think my already reduced supply of nervous energy was seriously affected and symptoms of nervous exhaustion began to show after I finished operational flying.

On a lighter note, it is probably not generally known that at times of severe stress or fright, usually both at once, on ground attack operations, the human sphincter (crudely referred to in the RAF as the 'ring-piece') goes through a series of contractions and relaxations. This phenomenon was given the name of sixpence/half-a-crown, and pilots at a debriefing after a heavy operation would say 'lots of sixpence/half-a-crown this time, and usually one pilot at least would say, 'I nibbled a bit out of my dinghy.' The folded dinghy was what we actually sat on in flight, the parachute being underneath it. The dinghy was fastened to the Mae West life jacket by a strap and a clip. If you were parachuting into water, the idea was to let your parachute go by hitting the release button about ten feet above the waves, then, as you fell, the strap pulled the dinghy open which then self-inflated from a CO_2 bottle in the pack and you climbed into it. We were all provided with a folding spike which looked like a pen-knife, the purpose of which was to stab the dinghy should it start to inflate while flying. It seldom happened but a few pilots lost their lives when their dinghy inflated in flight and they were pushed out of the aircraft.

The operations I have described so far were of course those in which I took part. Where there is a day's gap it would be when I left myself off the duty roster. On such days I would see the squadron off and then curl up on a pile of parachutes and cat-nap until their return. I can still do this though I doubt whether I would find it possible on a lumpy pile of parachutes.

Continuing our attacks, on 19 May we went to a target near Cherbourg and my note says, 'Bombed badly on wrong target, flak very thick and accurate.' On 20 May near Dieppe – 'Got a direct hit on a small bridge. Weather bad, no flak.' This I think must have been the 'trial' operation I spoke of earlier, to see if indeed we could find and destroy small targets. In the afternoon we attacked target No. 38 with my leading the squadron, with remarks 'Own bombing good, rest fair, little accurate heavy flak.' On 21 May I record one air-test and a low level cross-country flight and on 22 May smoke-laying practice. On 23 May we attacked radar at low level at Point de Percée and in the afternoon made a return visit to St Aubin for a low-level attack. Presumably our notion that we had destroyed it was false. The first of these two has my note, 'Lovely prang, target written off, no flak' and the second 'Even better, target written off. PO Jenkins hit but returned OK.' This junior officer became Squadron Leader Jenkins, CO of 257 Squadron, only a few weeks later.

The pilots' latrines were in a block of four with a front screen and divisions made of hessian, so using them was anything but private. A sloping channel with a constant flow of running water went underneath the seats and presumably discharged into a cesspit. Someone scrunched up a newspaper, lit it and dropped it into the channels outside the cubicles and was rewarded with howls of anguish one after the other as the occupants got their bottoms singed. It was not thought to be funny and was not repeated.

On 24 May we flew to Thorney Island again, from where we attacked a fuel dump south-west of Amiens. Rocket-firing Typhoons had already set it well alight, so we just put a load of bombs on the fire, after which flames came up to 2,000 feet and smoke to 10,000 feet. I could not imagine how much fuel it took to make such a blaze. One of our pilots thought he could fly through the smoke column just above the flames to see what it felt like. He was almost knocked out by his aircraft going up about 3,000 feet in three seconds and when he came to he was alarmed to see that a large number of rivets holding the aircraft skin to the airframe had gone missing. He flew back slowly and landed safely, but his aircraft was found to be a write-off with a cracked main wing-spar. What an idiot.

On 25 May we flew to Manston again from where we attacked marshalling yards at Valenciennes. My remarks show 'cloud obscured target, bombed Hazebrouck instead, good results.' There is then a gap in my logbook, perhaps a few days at home, but on 2 June we bombed the radar site at Cap d'Antifer which we had visited before when I did not drop my bombs. My notes say 'Bombing good, lots of light flak, target written off.' On 3 June we went to Thorney and back for some reason while on 5 June we bombed a radar site at St Valery-en-Caux, with the remark 'Bombing poor, some light flak.'

It was our practice to fly out on a given bearing for a given length of time, then to climb steeply aiming to cross the French coast at about 8,000 feet, which was just above the reach of 40 mm flak and just below the height at which the 88 mm could function. The Germans soon had their 40 mm guns firing to 10,000 feet and with such accuracy it was not possible to fly a fixed course for more than ten seconds without risking someone getting a direct hit. The big guns began to fire on low trajectories from a distance so they could have heavy flak bursting at quite a low level.

Once at height, wing manoeuvres became a bit complicated although after a while practice made perfect. A whole wing of three squadrons flew with the centre squadron (led by the wing commander) flying slightly ahead of the ones on each side. When an alteration of course was required (this could be pre-planned or caused by not making an accurate landfall) the wing commander would call over the radio 'starring' or 'porting', indicating a turn to the right or to the left respectively. With thirty-six aircraft spread over half a mile of sky, the squadron on the inside of the turn could not slow down enough while those on the outside could not go fast enough to maintain station. This was corrected by a 'cross-over' turn, where the inside squadron slid under the leading one coming up on the outside of it. The outside squadron climbed a little and crossed to the inside, thus getting everyone back in the right place. If the turn was protracted, the flights within each squadron could do their own 'cross-over'. It looked very fine when well executed, rather like an aerial ballet. On the run-up to a target the wing commander's squadron would take up station on the side nearest the target, then one by one the aircraft peeled over to dive on the target, followed by the other squadrons. Given accurate flying and diving, seventy-two 500 pound bombs would be dropped into quite a small area all in a couple of minutes. I would not like to be on the receiving end of such an attack.

We also had a routine for landing on our return. It was essential to get the aircraft on the ground for a check-over, refuelling and re-arming in as short a time as possible. This gave the ground staff the longest possible period in which to do their various jobs and to avoid the last squadron having to orbit the airfield more than once while waiting for other squadrons to land.

I am not quite sure whether I remember this correctly, but I believe that approaching the airfield each section of four aircraft changed from finger four formation to line astern, as it was not possible to circle the airfield in a spread-out formation, while line astern made manoeuvring easy. Circling was always anti-clockwise and the first squadron to land flew downwind, with the inside section sliding underneath and out to the right so the three sections were then in echelon to the right, parallel to the runway. The leader of the section would then turn 180° to his left with his section closely following him until he was flying down the length of the runway. Then he would pull up to his left, throttling back and dropping his undercarriage and flaps, with each aircraft doing the same at perhaps three-second intervals. Then each aircraft was dropped down on its final approach, landing closely one after the other and rolling to the end of the runway before turning off to its dispersal areas. Meanwhile the second section would arrive to do the same, then the third, each separated by perhaps five to six seconds, so that the last of the previous section had pulled up and away by the time the leader of the next section came in. This sounds slow, but actually, the whole wing of thirty-six aircraft would be down in under five minutes, each squadron doing exactly the same as the first one to land. I believe this routine was also used by the USAF, but I do not know who they copied it from. I suspect that the Americans developed the idea due to their liking for slick routines, which led to its general adoption by allied air forces.

As the wing commander had the only car on the camp, which was a big Ford estate car supplied by the RAF, when we had a trip out it was by truck with low metal sides and a canvas canopy. It was much more comfortable to sit on the side than on the floor, but if a bottom stuck out a little and the lorry brushed an overhanging tree, the bottom was whipped painfully. The floor it was. We went to Brockenhurst frequently and occasionally to Lymington. During a visit to Lymington after dark, the truck driver, for some reason, stopped and got out to go round the back of the truck. Unfortunately, he stood against the rear light. When the wing commander car came up behind the truck, the squadron leader who was driving it only saw the airman at the last second due to the hooded headlights. The airman was crushed against the truck. I was not present on that trip and so I do not know what action was taken. Presumably he was driven to the local hospital.

It was about this time that a flak battery with heavy guns was established a couple of fields away from us. The noise was deafening and made worse because this lot was using flashless ammunition and so there was no warning of the terrific bangs. How flashless powder functioned I had no idea.

On the evening of 5 June 1944 our wing commander told us that the next day, 6 June, would be D-Day and explained to us the basic invasion plans, which would rely on the battle-seasoned British and Commonwealth troops getting ashore on the left flank (led by airborne assault on the extreme left), and holding ground, which the British were good at, while the Americans piled ashore on the right with vast numbers of men and equipment. With an airborne assault on the extreme right, the whole of these armies would break out on the right and swing round, being anchored on the British positions.

To start with it did not go like that at all with the Americans. While the British airborne assault was totally successful in capturing and holding the vital bridge over the river Orne while our troops stormed ashore to their right, the American airborne assault was a shambles. Their 'tug' pilots met with a wall of flak and most of them didn't bother with finding the dropping zones but dropped the gliders and paratroopers and left the scene, while a few of them to their shame dropped their men without even reaching the shore. Meanwhile the troops to their left couldn't get off the beach.

We did not know this on D-Day itself. We went on an offensive recce behind the beachhead and the flight I was leading saw a line of horse-drawn covered wagons heading towards the beachhead. Not being at all sure what they were, I told my flight to orbit while I went down low to find out. Flying towards the column at fifty feet I could see a German soldier walking in front. He didn't see me until my aircraft was almost on top of him, then I saw his mouth open in a shout, whereupon about two dozen soldiers poured out of each wagon and dived into the ditches. This was fatal. We only had to strafe along the line of the ditches and we probably killed them all. Unfortunately we also hit some of the horses, while those pulling the front wagon broke loose and galloped off up the road.

Both going out on this trip and coming back, we could see that all the fields for miles around our airfield, which had been crammed with USA men and equipment, were now empty. It must have taken a miracle of organisation to move so much in such a short time and without getting all jammed up, but the Americans had a genius for complicated mass movement and I believe still have.

On 7 June we went to attack coastal guns at Longues but the army was not sure of the position, although I have forgotten what they meant. The guns were big enough. In the afternoon we went on another offensive recce and I saw what appeared to be a hay-cart, which might well have been French, although it was motorised, which seemed unlikely for a local. So I put in a few cannon shells and it blew up in a most spectacular manner, so evidently the hay was stuck on as camouflage. We saw lines of tanks and shot them up without visible effect and found another transport vehicle and set it on fire.

On 8 June we learned that the Americans were still stuck on the beach and it was a case of every aircraft attacking the German defenders to give the Americans a chance. We were ordered to destroy the small town of Isigny, a little inland, so we bombed in shallow dives at very low level and reduced a lot of it to rubble (thereby no doubt burying a lot of French civilians) and as I flew at chimney height over the little 'place de ville' I saw the town's fire-engine burning furiously outside its own fire-station. We used short delayed-action bombs on such attacks of perhaps ten seconds or so, enough to get a flight of four aircraft across the target while another flight would follow shortly.

I don't know if our efforts helped at all but the thousands of American soldiers we had seen crouching below the sand-dunes or low cliffs did get off the beach and silenced the nearby opposition. The airborne assault troops, after wandering around in small groups, eventually merged into a fighting force, so the invasion was back on track. On the same day we went out on recce again and shot up a line of tanks, again without visible effect although I suppose we must have killed some Germans caught outside their tanks. The tanks we were seeing were, I believe, of the 21st Panzer Group which had been stationed somewhere in the south. Hitler had said that these were not to be committed to battle without his direct orders. He and his staff thought that Normandy was a side-show and that the full invasion would occur at Calais. Eventually they were disabused of this idea and the German general, Rommel, phoned Hitler to plead with him to release the 21st Panzer Group, but Hitler's batman refused to wake him up so they lost several hours during which the Panzers might have caused mayhem. They lost many more hours through being unable to move during the day for fear of rocket attacks and having their night-time moves sabotaged by the French resistance.

For the most part we operated in small groups of four aircraft and even down to individuals attacking anything they could find. When flying just with my No. 2 I saw a German staff car speeding up a road which was cut into the side of a ravine. The road crossed the ravine on a high-arched bridge over which hung the crest of a large tree growing out of the side. The occupants of the car saw us and drove under the tree and stopped, hoping no doubt that we hadn't seen them. We shot through the tree top and the car burst into flames which we could see from the smoke. Later I learned that General Rommel had escaped from such an attack and so wondered whether it was him we so nearly killed.

On one of our operations soon after D-Day we flew over a marshalling yard which had had a heavy raid from Bomber Command. There was simply nothing left except for bits of railway sticking out of the ground. Usually railways were rapidly repaired but I doubt whether that one ever functioned again. On 10 June we went on an Army support operation near Fontenay, the target being in a wood apparently having its own flak battery which was of light calibre but very accurate, so much so that I had to weave the flight about and was unable to spot the target. I told my No. 3 to take over while I tried to silence the flak, which I did by diving on it vertically, firing my guns and letting my bombs go. It did the job but I don't know whether the rest of the flight hit the target.

When we returned to base after each operation we wrote in chalk on a blackboard what we had hit or destroyed. The wing commander looked at the board that day and said, 'Who attacked the flak position?' I said 'I did, Sir.' He looked at me and did not say any more, although he may have thought that I was showing the strain by doing such a crazy thing.

I have mentioned our wing commander several times without saying anything about him, which is unfair to the man who was after all our 'Big White Chief'. As far as I can remember his name was Baker. He was a big man and even then larger than life in his strong personality. He was a fighter type through and through and sported a handle-bar moustache to prove it. He always led us when the whole wing flew together, leading the squadrons alternately while the squadron CO stood down, as far as I remember. His call sign was 'Lochinvar', with the accent on the last syllable, and this suited him to a 'T'. Someone with a warped sense of humour at Fighter Command changed his call sign to 'Pooh-Bah'. He was furious and went on using 'Lochinvar' regardless. He probably enjoyed a high reputation with his seniors and so was able to get away with it.

I remember one amusing incident when the whole wing was returning from an operation, when our CO, Squadron Leader Ronnie Fokes must have been day-dreaming and allowed 257 Squadron to get a little ahead of the squadron the wing commander was leading. Suddenly over the intercom came the message 'Ronnie, who is leading this lot, you or me?' Our CO must have come to with a start. He throttled back and dropped his radiator flap, which acted as an air-brake, which he certainly shouldn't have done, and we all shot past him. We soon sorted ourselves out but I imagine the wing commander had words with our CO afterwards.

12 June was a bad day. We split up into flights on an offensive recce and my remarks were 'Bombed engine shed, bomb did not go off. Damaged one transport, flak!!!' My other note says 'Squadron Leader Fokes missing.' He was hit and seen to bail out but he may have been over the area occupied by 21st Panzer Divison which probably used him for target practice. We were shattered and when the wing commander asked me what had happened I said, 'I don't know Sir, I wasn't there.' After debriefing he asked me to stay behind, when he said, 'Smithy, you knew Ronnie and his wife well, didn't you?' (How on earth did he know that?) I said, 'Yes, I did,

Sir.' He said, 'Take my car and go and see Audrey (Ronnie's wife), then go home to your wife for the night.' Fortunately Audrey was very calm so the visit was not too distressing and, of course, I enjoyed a trip home.

Trying to get back to base travelling down the A34 (then just a country road) I came up against an Army convoy miles long and I could see myself spending hours getting back. An Army despatch rider pulled up alongside and shouted, 'Are you in a hurry, Sir?' When I shouted, 'Yes!' he said, 'Follow me' and set off at over sixty mph down the outside of the convoy and, terrified by this as I was, I had no alternative but to keep up with him and came out just short of Winchester to my great relief.

At this stage of events my memory lets me down completely. We lost Wing Commander Baker on 16 June, only four days after losing our own CO, Squadron Leader Fokes, but for some reason I have completely forgotten about this shattering event and neither do I remember Wing Commander Baldwin, DSO, DFC and bar, taking command of the wing. I am indebted to Norman Franks in his book *Typhoon Attack* for putting me right on this score. He also writes that Wing Commander Baker called on his radio for the wing to turn 180° (in effect to return to base) and immediately following this he crashed. I was flying that day but was only airborne for ten minutes when an aircraft fault made me return to base so I would not have heard the instruction.

Having forgotten about the death of the wing commander, I do remember a consequence of it. My first wedding anniversary was due on 26 June and I wanted a twenty-four hour pass to meet my wife in Basingstoke, which was not too difficult to get to for either of us. I wrote out an application for this pass and was obliged to give it to the senior surviving officer, who was the CO of 197 Squadron. I have indicated what I thought of him earlier in the story and true to form he said, 'I'm not going to read that. Get it typed.' (As far as I know, there was no rule requiring applications for leave to be typed.) I said, I 'can't type, Sir' and so he said, 'Do it with one finger then.'

I tried but I am useless on anything operated by keys. So I bribed our clerk with twenty Player cigarettes to do it for me. Once done, I gave it to the CO again. This time he read it and said, 'Good old Smithy,' grinning all the while. I could have hit him, but at least I got my leave. My wife, meanwhile, was scouring Basingstoke for a room for the night and she finally found a couple willing to let us sleep (but not all night of course) in the attic. As long as we had a bed we couldn't have cared less about it being in the attic. Next morning they gave us a decent breakfast, which we needed.

Before returning to operations with 146 Wing, I think it is worth emphasising that the whole responsibility of getting over 5,000 vessels from all the ports in southern England and Wales to the Normandy beaches, including towing the enormous concrete caissons which were sunk at the beach-heads to make the 'Mulberry Harbours' and laying a fuel pipeline all the way, was that of the Royal Navy, which as ever accomplished it to perfection. There was a 'Command' ship from which the Senior Naval Officer supervised the extraordinarily complex operation and on which there were senior officers representing the Army, the RAF and presumably the US Forces acting as liaison, using radio frequencies by means of which they could contact and be contacted as such by our wing. This was not only to keep the various commanders in step but also to avoid 'friendly' fire, although the latter did not always manage to avoid mistakes costly to service lives.

Soon after D-Day we started to hear voices speaking in unaccented English directing us to change course or other instructions different from those we had been briefed on. It did not sound right and I don't think anyone was fooled by it. However, this must have been anticipated because within days some gadgets were delivered for fitting into the wing commander and squadron leader aircrafts. These had a slot across the front through which little tumblers could be seen, about twelve of them I think, which were faceted with symbols on each facet. At a signal from base the little tumblers rotated and stopped to show a message that could be understood from the symbols. The messages could neither be intercepted nor jammed, but whether in the end they had to be used, I do not know.

Another change which took place at about this time was the fitting of armour plating under the prominent radiator and under the pilot's seat. Until then the only armour plate had been behind the pilot as was usual in fighter aircraft. This change took place against a background of severe losses of Typhoons from flak puncturing the radiator and causing coolant loss leading to engine seizure within minutes. Pilots were also being injured or killed by splinters of exploding flak coming up through the seat. The one problem with carrying all the extra weight was that the aircraft took a lot longer to pull out from a dive-bombing attack. This carried it closer to the guns which were firing at it and thereby actually increased the possibilities of being hit. After a few attacks carrying the extra armour, I disliked the handling of the aircraft so much that I had it all taken out of my own aircraft. Whether it was subsequently put back after I left, I have no idea.

An amusing incident occurred when we were off duty and some of us were bathing as best we could, when a gaggle of girls arrived at the gate leading onto our airfield, hoping perhaps to talk to some fighter pilots. They were quite unprepared to see a number of naked men and fled squealing. I assume that they came from a neighbouring farm.

During one of the many operations I have listed I was leading one section of four aircraft when a flak battery which we didn't know was there opened up and hit No. 4, who started to drop back. No. 3 dropped back to be with him so I called out, 'Red 3, Red 1, come back here.' (I use the colour Red but it might have been Blue or Green or Brown, or our wing commander's favourite Purple or Puce.) After some hesitation No. 3 came back into formation, then I called, 'Red 4, Red 1, I hope you make a good landing and the best of luck, Red 1 – out.' He answered something and was obviously badly frightened and I could not hear what he said. Strangely I did not put his name in my logbook.

When we got back I summoned my flight together and said, 'While I am leading, anyone who is hit is on his own, including me. The Germans would love to get two for the price of one. You cannot do anything for the one who is hit, and the formation cannot afford to lose another one, thus reducing its firepower.' Someone said, 'That's a bit rough' so I said, 'It's a rough business' and that concluded the discussion. It was quite different if the aircraft in trouble was over water, when another would stay to report his position and fly around as long as he could so that a good fix could be obtained on his location for air-sea rescue to pick him up.

We did not get another CO for about ten days during which time I led the squadron to the best of my ability. Immediately after my return from visiting Audrey Fokes and spending twenty-four hours at home, I found the squadron going slack and discipline poor. I told the office staff to go outside so that I could speak to the pilots privately. I said words to the effect that they had got slack because they thought there was no CO to keep them in line, but there was always a CO and until further notice that was me and I told them to pull themselves together. This improved things a lot but, as I did not have the rank, a commanding personality or an incisive mind, it was difficult. I wondered whether the delay in appointing a new CO was because the wing commander wanted to see what sort of job I could do. For one operation we went into the briefing tent and, without warning, he said to me, 'Brief them.' Not even knowing what the operation was to be before going into the tent made it difficult, but brief them I did.

While under my command 257 Squadron went out on 15 June to support the Army east of Caen when we dive-bombed a small wood. My remarks were 'Excellent show. Bags of flak.' A raid on 16 June was aborted while on 17 June we went on 'armed recce', bombed a bridge which we missed and my remark was 'Waste of time.' On 20 June we went to bomb a target east of Boulogne and managed to bomb the wrong one, but destroyed one building with a little light flak.

Flight Lieutenant Kistler was lost. He had acquired a reputation, partly because he was from the USA and stayed with the RAF instead of joining the US Army Airforce, and partly because, in spite of strict instructions not to attempt a belly-landing on a wire mesh runway, he did it anyway. His guns dug under the wire and his aircraft flipped onto its back. The fire engine immediately doused it in thick foam and Kistler was dragged out almost drowned in foam. He seemed all right then started to shake uncontrollably. It was the only time I saw someone going into extreme shock.

Also on 20 June we dive-bombed something or other and on 24 June we went low-level bombing west of Lisieux. I saw the end of a train going into a tunnel so broke away, went down to twenty feet and flew up the railway, letting my bombs go at the last moment then pulling up sharply. The bombs bounced into the tunnel; then, as I flew past the tunnel ventilator, a solid column of black smoke and bits and pieces of the train shot up. I thought it would take a lot of work to clear that tunnel. I rejoined the squadron which I was leading but have no further notes as to what else we might have hit.

That day our new CO arrived. He had previously been on 197 Squadron when I was there and had been quite popular, but unfortunately he complied with the Peter Principle by being promoted to his own level of incompetence. He seemed to be barely literate and the other flight commander and myself had to do the squadron paper work which he seemed incapable of doing himself. He had to defer to me for information and any necessary action and I rapidly came to despise him and probably showed it. His unpopularity on 257 Squadron caused friction with 197 Squadron members who knew him in his previous position and could not understand why we disliked him so much.

His leadership in the air was no better, at least on the few occasions I flew with him. The day after his arrival we went off armed with a long-range tank under one wing and a single 500-pound bomb under the other. This was on 25 June 1944 and we were going on a deep penetration to bomb a reinforced concrete bridge at Beaumont le Roger. On the way out the CO said, 'Drop tanks' just as we were passing over HMS *Rodney*, an old battleship with nine 16 inch guns (all pointing forward) which was trying to destroy a heavy German concrete gun position which British troops had by-passed. The Navy had a rooted objection to having things dropped on it, particularly when they look like bombs, and *Rodney* let fly with its entire anti-aircraft armament and we had a couple of scary minutes until we were out of range.

As we passed over the French coast I caught sight of a little 'spotter' plane flying up and down over the German concrete gun emplacement, presumably directing *Rodney*'s fire, and at that moment a 16 inch shell went right into the emplacement and caused a great explosion (the shells weigh over a ton). Subsequently on our way back the German heavy gun was lying on its side pointing at nowhere. It had previously hit a tanker off-shore and this was still blazing, but that wouldn't happen again.

We went on our way and the bridge we were after came into view from miles away. To hit this sort of bridge requires an attacking approach of about 45°, at which angle there is little, if any, gap between the bridge pillars so you cannot help but hit it. Our new CO made no attempt to do this and came in at 70°–80° when you have a pillar perhaps two feet thick then fifty feet of open space to the next pillar so nearly all the bombs went straight under the bridge and exploded on the far side. I was carrying a twelve-hour delay bomb (the fusing is set on the ground before the aircraft takes off) but it exploded on impact when I was only fifty feet up and I only survived because I actually hit a pillar on its end and, while I heard a mighty bang, I was protected from the blast and shrapnel by the decking of the bridge as I passed over it. Had the bomb gone under the bridge I would have been blown out of the sky. The damage to the bridge was minimal so the busy traffic it carried for the Germans during the night continued unabated. Shortly after our effort I believe a Lancaster bomber, carrying an 'earthquake' bomb and heavily escorted with fighters, dropped its single bomb (these super-heavy bombs could be dropped with pin-point accuracy). The bridge simply disappeared.

When I got back I said to our new CO that I didn't think it was a good idea to drop tanks when passing over HMS *Rodney* but he said he hadn't seen it. I also complained to the wing commander that my delayed action bomb had exploded on impact and could have killed me. He burst out laughing and said, 'Hard luck, Smithy.' A few days later the same thing happened to him and all hell broke loose, but then he was the wing commander. It led to the withdrawal of a batch of delayed-action bombs in which the brittle plastic Bakelite had been used in an attempt to save metal but the plastic shattered upon impact. I formed the opinion that as soon as our new CO had found his feet he would get rid of me rather than keep a senior flight commander who thought little of him. However, things remained as they were for another ten days or so.

On 29 June I led the squadron again on an armed recce in the Lisieux-Argentan area. We split into pairs or even singles and found only two trucks to shoot up. Returning alone I saw a line of German staff cars drawn up outside a small château and thought a few dozen cannon shells would make them sit up and take notice, so I turned towards the château but turned too much and, as I started to correct this, I realised I was about to hit the ground. My life did not flash before me in the approved manner; I just thought, 'You've killed yourself, you silly prick.' I pulled back on the stick and, much to my surprise, the propeller did not touch the ground, my aircraft shot past the end of the château level with the ground-floor windows, and I gave myself such a fright I just flew home with my heart pounding nineteen to the dozen.

After returning from one of the recent sorties, we had been debriefed and were on our way to our tents when a corporal came up to me and said, 'Would you come and have a look at your aircraft, Sir?' I said, 'What is the matter with it, Corporal?' and he replied, 'I would rather show you, Sir.' So I went with him and he got underneath the wings and pointed upwards. I went under also and saw the rifling marks of a German heavy flak shell right across my aircraft. Had I been banking in the opposite direction that would have been a direct hit and I would not have come back.

On 30 June we went on another armed recce in the same area and my notes read 'Saw nothing, bombed railway and missed.' On 3 July we flew to Hurn, north of Bournemouth, in anticipation of operating from France and on the same day we went low-level bombing of railway sidings at St Montfort when I wrote 'Bombing good, hits on sidings, much finger trouble in squadron.' This expression meant that the squadron was making a mess of its attacks in one way or another. The expression 'pull your finger out' was a common one in the RAF, when drawing attention to something that was not being done properly. I'm glad this did not happen when I was acting CO.

On 6 July we went on another armed recce, my remarks being 'Bombed woods, no result seen.' That afternoon I led the squadron for the last time where I note 'Direct hit on transport, weather foul, some flak.' On 7 July we went to dive-bomb some crossroads near Bernay and my remarks were 'Bombing good, no flak, Flt. Sgt. Blair killed.' There must have been some flak which I did not see but which hit Flt. Sgt. Blair, who often flew as my No. 2. He bailed out but his parachute did not open and I saw him plummetting to earth. I don't like to think about what must have been going through his mind as he realised he was a dead man.

On 8 July we flew to airfield B15 near Bayeux in Normandy, but while the wire mesh strip had been laid, nothing else was ready so, after a walk round and listening to one of 'Monty's' great gun barrages, we flew back to Hurn. On my return I found that, as expected, I had been posted away. I made no attempt to get myself a squadron billet elsewhere. I had flown just sixty trips over the murderous countryside of northern France and was quite extraordinarily lucky to be alive. I think, of course, that I would have made a much better CO than the man who got the job but then I am alive and he isn't. Had I been made squadron leader I do not think that I would have survived and my nerves would have collapsed before they actually did.

This was the end of my fighting career. The 'Silver Lining' now showed broadly across the allied effort to get rid of Nazi Germany and, although there were many hard battles to come and casualties to be suffered, the end was no longer in doubt. I do not remember making any farewells as I left 257 Squadron but no doubt I must have shaken a few hands. Probably the aircraft were away on operation at the time I actually left, but someone found time to go through my kit and steal my sleeping bag, which was annoying as I still needed one on my posting when I was under canvas.

At Brockenhurst our departure became imminent for a move to Hurn, preparatory to going to France. We asked if we could use the village hall for a farewell party. The local council officials said they would be delighted, having no idea what they were letting themselves in for, but then neither did I. We bought nine barrels of beer, each of nine gallons. I persuaded an uncle of mine who worked for Booth's Gin to supply a crate of mixed spirits. The beer was delivered by train a few days in advance and we rolled the barrels the short distance from the train to the hall. My job was to tour round and find enough females to go round and also some food. I found plenty of willing service women but the only food was a Dundee cake about three-feet square, which I collected from an army camp.

Some days before the party was due to take place, we were in The Rose and Crown and talking to the local chief constable about this and that. I took the opportunity to ask him if I could get my wife to the party, in view of the fact that the whole south coast had become a forbidden area for ten miles inland, except of course for local people. The officer said that this was no problem. He was not worried about a few wives. I wrote to my wife and asked her to travel down by train and I would meet her at Brockenhurst station. This she did but we found that the chief constable had not informed his officers to let us through. The policeman at the barrier flatly refused to let my wife off the station and in the end she had to wait for a London train to come in, travel to Victoria, across to Paddington then to Oxford, where she walked five miles home carrying her luggage and without any food or drink. She was shattered.

The party itself was more of an orgy than anything else. We inexpertly tapped the beer barrels which made the floor wet and, with a mixture of Dundee cake, made a terrible mess. Everybody, except those involved in serving, got extremely drunk and then apparently went outside for copulation and the area was strewn with condoms (then called French letters) some of which someone had rolled onto the horns of the few cows in a small field at the back. When it was all over we locked up and slunk away, ashamed of the way the generosity of the local people had been abused.

To conclude the Typhoon story, when the squadrons moved to France (I had left the squadron before this) I was told that often a Typhoon would be dispatched to Tangmere or other permanent airfields, carrying empty drop tanks, one with a detachable nosecone. By prior arrangement with the airfield concerned, the empty drop tank would be filled with twelve gallons of beer while the other one was stuffed with chocolates and cigarettes. This kept the pilots in France in a good frame of mind, but for how long this was continued I don't know.

Chapter 13

Test Pilot

My posting was to 84 Group Support Unit (GSU for short) and this was stationed at Thruxton near Andover (now a motor-cycle race track, I believe). The function of the group was to test all new and repaired aircraft for fitness to fly and fight and to deliver them to the squadrons at airfields in Northern France. A small group of four test pilots (of which I became one) did all the testing while other pilots did the ferrying. We functioned from different dispersed sites and really only met in the officers' mess after finishing for the day. All the pilots lived under canvas but, as I had a tent to myself, this was no hardship in the warm weather. Washing and bathing facilities were available in the mess, likewise toilets, and the tents were close by the mess. It was a great deal more comfortable than the airfield I had just left.

I arrived late one morning and was directed to the mess where I was enjoying a pint of beer sitting on a windowsill when I was suddenly thumped on the back and a voice said, 'I'd know that back anywhere.' This was my old CO from two previous service positions, Wing Commander Watkins. I was delighted to be serving under him again and he seemed very pleased to see me. He allocated me to the test-flight of which the CO was Squadron Leader 'Dicky' Martin DFC, a very experienced officer (he subsequently went on to test the delta-wing fighters being developed in the 1950s). There were two other pilots: the first was a wonderful flier but had no idea of what made an aircraft work, and the other, who was in a bad state of nerves, killed himself by flying into a hill-top in bad weather. Some pilots whose nerves had gone seemed compelled to press on regardless, often with fatal consequences.

I went with the CO to the scene of the crash and listened to civilian witnesses saying the aircraft exploded in the air or something equally false, in spite of the long crash marks on the ground showing that the aircraft had impacted at a very shallow angle and had torn itself to pieces as it ploughed along killing the pilot. (Many civilian witnesses to accidents invent the most outrageous stories. Their purpose in doing so escapes me.) So that left only three pilots and we flew various types of Spitfires, Typhoons and the occasional USAF P51, which we called the Mustang. It is to my eternal regret that I did not get round to flying one of these wonderful aircraft during my time there.

There was certainly no 'Holywood' glamour about the job of test pilot that we had. It was a daily grind of up to five test flights per day, which always included a trip to the south coast where we tested the guns by firing into the sea off Chesil Beach. The average trip was about forty-five minutes but sometimes only ten to fifteen minutes if the aircraft behaved badly and was obviously in need of further work. Then we got back on the ground as quickly as possible. Looking back I think that it was a pity that I was not given a desk job for a while. I would have hated it but my increasingly nervous condition could have benefited from a complete break from flying.

There were a few incidents to liven things up. On one occasion the armourers were loading up rockets with dummy heads (made of concrete) in a Typhoon. They had just hung the first one and moved off to get another one and an airman of a different trade was in the cockpit. He was probably an 'instrument basher' (why men of this trade were called 'bashers' escapes me; rough treatment is not something one gives to instruments) but whoever he was he managed to touch the rocket-firing button and the rocket roared off across the airfield but mercifully did not hit anyone. By the grace of God, the armourers had moved away, otherwise they would have been badly burnt. Thereafter rockets were not loaded unless the cockpit was empty, at least on our unit.

I was sitting at the office desk one day with my back to the open window when a machine gun suddenly opened up. By reflex action I flung myself over backwards to get below window height and then the gun stopped. Peering over the window sill I saw a very sick-looking armourer tottering about behind the wing of a Mustang where he had been checking the 0.5 inch Browning guns. This gun looks very similar to the 0.303 guns usually used by the RAF, although of course larger and heavier, but they had one important difference, which the armourer either didn't know or had forgotten. The 0.303 gun could be 'cocked' rather liked a revolver with a breech-block held back in the latch (called a rear-sear) but the 0.5 gun could not, as it did not have a rear-sear. The armourer pulled the breach-block back with a toggle but instead of staying back its strong spring slammed it forward making the gun fire and because the man held onto his toggle the gun continued to fire until he recovered his wits and let go of it. In the meantime he had been flying backwards and forwards like a rag doll. The heavy bullets went across the airfield and came down on the admin buildings, the occupants of which were not amused, but no real damage was done. I expect the armourer got a heavy ticking off but nothing worse.

Our test flight possessed a jeep, which for some reason I drove about on errands on which the flight commander sent me as his senior pilot. I did not drive sedately as would have been suitable in the camp but careered about at high speed. This apparently was reported to Wing Commander Watkins who on a visit to our dispersal said, 'Smithy, if you go on driving like this I'll take the jeep away.' One warning was enough and thereafter I behaved myself driving.

There was an event, amusing in retrospect but not at the time, when I was away at another camp for some reason which I have long forgotten. The camp had the ubiquitous Nissan huts for sleeping purposes which were made out of corrugated iron and were uninsulated, resulting in temperatures high enough to bake a cake in the heat of summer and cold enough to cause hypothermia in the winter unless you slept fully dressed. There was a pot-bellied stove in the centre, which fortunately was not lit. Presumably I had had a few pints of beer during the evening and had to get up to relieve myself in the middle of the night. I got out of the door without incident but upon my return I set the wrong course for my bed in the darkness and crashed into the stove, which I knocked over. I narrowly missed being guillotined by the cast iron chimney, which, bereft of the support of the back of the stove, slid down through the hole in the roof and hit the concrete fire base with a mighty clang. Of course it woke the whole hut and probably the ones on either side, but apart from bruises I was unharmed.

It was not very long after I started as test pilot that I blotted my copybook by pulling the wheels of a Spitfire up before being properly airborne. The aircraft sank down while the propeller chewed itself to pieces on the runway, then flopped onto its belly. I went along a hundred yards or so in a cloud of smoke and sparks. The ambulance and fire tender came tearing up but neither was needed. A truck pulled the wreckage off the runway onto the grass where it could be dismantled and taken away. I swore at the time that the engine had failed and said so to Wing Commander Watkins. 'Oh no, it didn't, Smithy, you pulled the wheels up too soon' was his reaction, and of course he was right, but he didn't create too much fuss.

Some of the flying was dangerous in the extreme. The test pilot who was such a good flier came down in a Typhoon with his normally ruddy face looking very pale. He said that the Typhoon that he had been flying had locked its controls in a high speed dive, which was usually the concluding exercise in an air-test, and he had used all his strength pulling on the stick and narrowly missed diving straight into the ground. I had been made the resident Typhoon expert by reason of my experience and Dicky Martin said, 'It's your job, Smithy.' So I took it up and did what the other pilot had done with the same result, except that I was forewarned, so tried to pull out of the dive sooner than he had. Even so I had to put both feet on the dashboard and both hands on the stick pulling for all I was worth and eventually the aircraft levelled out with some height to spare. I flew back and after landing I said to the chief, 'No one is to fly that aircraft again until I say so.'

I got to thinking about when Ronnie Fokes had showed me over a Typhoon in its early days. I remembered that the 'balance' weight found on a little platform on the front of the stick (it was a lump of lead bolted to the platform) on all fighter aircraft, including the suicidal one, had initially been fitted onto the elevator bar in Typhoons. The function of this weight was to act against the pilot if he tried to pull too many 'gs' and risk breaking the airframe. When the extra straps to strengthen a Typhoon's tail were fitted, the weights on the elevator bar had been removed in favour of the weight in front of the stick. I asked the chief how old the aircraft was and he looked up its service record and said it was an old one and must have been rebuilt into a Typhoon 1B from a 1A. So I said, 'You've got two balance weights in that aircraft.' He didn't believe me but I had a bet with him. We had a very diminutive corporal on the flight and after removing the aircraft radio we pushed the corporal into the hatch armed with a torch and a spanner (in spite of his loud protests). He clanked around in the back of the fuselage then a little later pushed a balance weight on its moment arm out of the hatch and we pulled him out after it. So I won my bet (which I didn't take) and subsequently the aircraft behaved normally.

I've made a long story out of this but the question which remained was how this aircraft had been flown for nearly three years without someone reporting its dangerous fault, or perhaps reports were made but, there being nothing visibly wrong with it, no one took any notice of the complaints. My otherwise 'patchy' memory served me well on that occasion.

Wing Commander Watkins flew himself over to France and borrowed a jeep to drive up to the front line, where he met up with a Canadian division waiting to attack outside Caen. The RAF was supposed to fly over and bomb the enemy in front of the Canadians before the attack went in and after a short while they could be seen approaching. The wing commander suddenly got a feeling that all was not well, so he said to the Canadian officer, 'Must be off, old boy, best of luck' and then drove away. This was just as well because, somewhere along the line, the RAF were given incorrect map references with the result that many bombs were dropped amongst the Canadians.

The clothes I wore for the day's work could not by any stretch of the imagination be regarded as suitable for an RAF officer. They consisted of khaki trousers and jacket (brought back from Malta) liberally splashed with black and white paint from the time on 257 Squadron when we had to paint our own aircraft with the black and white stripes common to all Allied aircraft, topped up with a bright pink, silk lace scarf (also from Malta) which was wound several times around my neck with the ends tucked inside my jacket. I must have looked an absolute fright but the wing commander only once passed a remark. When I came into the mess tent for breakfast he said, 'Here comes Smithy, the acme of sartorial grace.' Why he put up with one of his officers dressed as I was I don't know.

I caused no little stir when one day returning from a gun test I saw storm clouds over the South Downs, so, rather than risk going under them close to the ground, I landed at Worthy Down, a little Fleet Air Arm base, to wait for the storm to pass, having radioed base to this effect so they wouldn't think I had gone missing. Worthy Down is on the top of a hill and I didn't realise how much the ground sloped up. When I touched down, my aircraft bounced twenty feet into the air. Giving the engine a burst of power to prevent it stalling, I then landed safely and taxied up to the watch tower, where I switched off, got out and went in to apologise for my dreadful landing. They thought nothing of it, as three-point landings were not in their repertoire for flying on carriers. The officer of the watch was very nice and, pretending not to notice my scarecrow appearance, he invited me to the 'wardroom' for lunch – very brave of him. All the smartly dressed naval officers also pretended not to notice and treated me right royally and with impeccable manners. Subsequently I took off again and beat up the airfield at full power to show my appreciation.

I have already said that aircraft faults sometimes caused serious frights, and one in particular which I remember was when I was flying a Spitfire south for a gun test and the gun panels on the left side came undone on the rear edge and stood up. This caused the aircraft to slew to the left and start to roll. I corrected this but found I couldn't control the aircraft below about 120 mph which is 30 mph higher than normal landing speed. I was near a large airfield so I did a tail-up landing (the brakes cannot be used until the tail drops) and managed to pull up before running off the end of the runway. I taxied up to the watchtower, got out and requested the services of a mechanic. He came quickly, fastened the spring-loaded screws on the gun panels and said, 'There we are, Sir'.

I took off and the panels immediately came undone again. I flew along with the left wing tip a few inches off the ground and held the aircraft down, at great risk, to get enough speed to make it controllable. I survived this and flew back to Thruxton where I had to do another tail-up landing. Thruxton's runway was none too long but I managed to turn off the end of the runway at some risk to the undercarriage as the aircraft swerved round.

On the subject of runways, Thruxton had another one that was very short and not normally used. I did use it once when flying a Typhoon but cannot remember whether I was instructed to try landing on it or chose to use it, rather than divert elsewhere, due to the main runway being blocked upon my return from a test flight. I made an approach about 10 mph slower than usual with a lot of power and the nose of the aircraft held up. Upon clearing the airfield boundary, I shut the throttle and more or less stalled the aircraft into the ground. Then, using the brakes, I had no problem stopping well before the end of the runway. I reported to the controller that, given an approach in the manner I used, there was no reason why the runway should not be used if it was necessary. The controller passed this information on to the squadron leader of the delivery/collection flight who said that on no account should any of his pilots try such an approach, which he thought was particularly dangerous. It made no difference to me one way or the other, but the squadron leader probably thought that some pilots lacked the finer skills necessary to do this safely.

Having survived two major incidents and numerous minor alarms, I was beginning to feel the strain, although this was greatly relieved when, sitting in the mess after lunch (properly dressed for a change), I heard the wing commander shouting, 'Where's Smithy?' I stood up and put my head out of the open window and said, 'I'm here, Sir,' and remained standing as he obviously had something to say to me. He came in with a piece of paper in one hand and two sticks of chalk in the other. With the chalk he drew stripes of the colours of the DFC upon my battledress under my wings and gave me the piece of paper which was a telegram from the Air Officer Commanding (AOC for short) of 84 Group congratulating me on the award of the DFC, and from the AOC of 2nd Tactical Air Force doing the same. I still have these and must take steps to preserve them, as they are now very tattered.

Needless to say the award led to a boozy celebration in the mess that night, although I have no recollection other than waking up in my tent with a considerable hangover. I got some sneering remarks from the squadron leader from 197 Squadron, who visited us for some reason and who, I suppose, was jealous. He had been on Typhoon operations longer than me but up to then had been an instructor in Canada, while I had served the better part of two years on Spitfire operations previously.

One of the most amusing recollections I have of Thruxton is eating meals in the mess tent with the sides rolled up on account of the hot weather. This meant sharing the tent with swarms of wasps which came in for a good feed. This did not faze me at all. If you ignore them you come to no harm, but others did not feel the same way at all and seemed to spend more of the meal time thrashing about to beat the insects off than enjoying their meal. These days one might see a couple of wasps all summer. What a difference.

In the officers' mess we were very lucky to have a professional chef who came out of the kitchen to carve the joints. He would say, 'Outside or inside (of the joint), Sir' and carve accordingly. His meals were a revelation in what can be done with service food.

R.A.F. Form 683.

SECRET.

CYPHER MESSAGE.

(L 12842-10346). Wt. 24367-1348. 246M. 8/43. T.S. 70
(L 14129-10346). Wt. 50714-8743. 200M. 2/44 T.S. 700

WARNING. This cypher message must first be paraphrased if it is necessary to publish its text or to communicate it to persons outside British Government Services and Departments. Messages marked "O.T.P." are excepted from this rule.

FROM— 257 (Burma) Squadron.	CENTRAL REGISTRY REF SR 21 SEP 1944 84 GROUP SUPPORT UNIT	Date 21st Sept.	
To— 84 G.S.U.		Time of Receipt 211425	Despatch 211559
REPEATED—		System TP	HAND

Serial No. 901-30in

P.10 14th Sept.

Signals 31st August from A.E.A.F. to this Unit " Personal from A.O.C.-in-C. to F/Lt. R.G. Smith D.F.C. Many congratulations on your award of the D.F.C. - Leigh-Mallory "

T.O.O. 141405(B)

ACTION COPY

Ref: 84G/S.2211/2/P.1/Pers.

Headquarters,
No.84 Group,
ROYAL AIR FORCE.

30th August, 1944.

Dear Smith.

I want to extend to you my warm congratulations upon the award to you of the Distinguished Flying Cross. It was thoroughly well earned and deserved.

Wishing you good luck and further success.

Yours sincerely
L O Brown

(L. O. BROWN.)
Air Vice-Marshal,
Commanding,
No.84 Group, R.A.F.

Flight Lieutenant R. G. Smith, D.F.C.,
No.84 Group Support Unit.

Copies of signals received upon the author's award of the DFC

Before moving on I will mention the small monthly magazine called *TEE EM*, copies of which were handed out to units around the country. It contained news and views and drew attention to important topics and there were also amusing stories, some of them based on Pilot Officer Percy Prune (the silliest and most useless pilot in the RAF) and his dog Binder. These stories were illustrated by cartoons and were always good for a laugh. The cartoonist was called Fougasse and was quite famous in his day. Each month there was an article headed 'The Most Highly Derogatory Order of the Irremovable Finger' and the article described the most stupid thing that anyone had done in the previous month, as far as the authors could tell. Some were almost beyond belief. I have mentioned 'finger trouble' and 'pull your finger out' as standard expressions of not doing things right in the RAF. The USAF equivalent was 'pull your thumb out of your ass' and still seems to be in use today, according to some films. The extreme unlikelihood of anyone having his finger (or thumb) up his ass only adds weight to these expressions.

There was one report in *TEE EM*, which I shall never forget and it concerned the agonising death of a young airwoman. Some idiot put a 'Very light' cartridge into a lighted stove in a dispersal hut. These cartridges had a strong propellant charge in them which, when fired from a special hand gun, threw an incandescent light a hundred feet into the air for signal purposes. On this occasion the cartridge exploded, blowing the stove open, and the incandescent light went straight into the airwoman's open mouth. What she must have suffered before she died does not bear thinking about, but, as a result of this 'prank', putting anything explosive into a lighted stove became, I believe, a Court martial offence.

The other incident which occurred at Thruxton was an officers' mess party. My wife came down from Oxford and booked a room for both of us at a local hotel, and I went to fetch her in the test-flight jeep. The carrying of civilians in service vehicles was forbidden and so, while no one would question me on the way to Andover, there was a risk of being stopped by Military Police with my wife in the jeep on the way back. So I stopped for a bunch of soldiers thumbing a lift and they piled in. I said, 'Sit close to my wife, please; she isn't supposed to be here.' They didn't mind a bit, so they sat close around and I took off at high speed for Thruxton. One of them said, 'He still thinks he's in his bloody Spitfire' and after a while they asked me to put them down at the crossroads. I have no idea whether that is really where they wanted to go or whether they were too frightened by my driving to take any more.

We arrived in the mess in good shape and, as usual, my wife was surrounded by young officers and danced with many of them. In my usual stance I propped up the bar (I am not a jealous person) and a good time was had by all. The only puzzle was how we got back to the hotel. I'm sure that I was too drunk to drive the jeep, although in spite of this I didn't want to be caught in the early hours with a civilian female passenger. Somebody must have driven us back and I would not be surprised if the wing commander had fetched a sober airman to drive his car for us. A military policeman would hesitate to stop a senior officer's car even with a passenger aboard.

I reached the stage where I longed for bad weather so no flying was possible, but of course it only made the workload heavier trying to catch up when the weather cleared and so my nervous condition continued to deteriorate. I reported sick. I told the station senior medical officer of how I was getting into the habit of screaming at misbehaving aircraft and hitting the canopy with my fist, a loss of control which I did not like at all. The stupid MO made a very amateur show of laughing it off, presumably having no idea what to do about it (it was his main duty to watch for signs of nervous distress among aircrew). I asked for a posting to a less stressful job.

Before leaving No. 84 GSU behind, a bit more about Wing Commander Watkins. He was everything I expected of a senior officer, educated (Public School for sure), articulate and effortless in command, which I both admired and envied. He was also 'gentlemanly', an old fashioned quality for which I have always had a high regard, but one most conspicuous by its absence in many of the officers who made senior rank during the war. Others may have had different views of Wing Commander Watkins but I was both pleased and proud to have served under him in three different units.

I was posted to No. 3 TEV at the end of September 1944. The station was called Aston Down and was situated on top of a hill above the 'Golden Valley' in Gloucestershire, an area of great natural beauty which afforded some beautiful walks and where the then disused Thames-Severn canal was situated (now partly restored, I believe). The nearby local town of any size was Stroud, about which I remember very little except that one evening, when a group of us went there, there was an RAF lorry parked half in the road and half on the pavement right outside a hotel. We asked the driver who was sitting at the wheel to move down the road a little and he refused. This led to one of our number opening the driver's door and threatening to throw him into the street and drive the lorry away himself, at which point the driver agreed to move the lorry, no doubt adding to his store of anti-officer feelings. I have thought about this but cannot come up with any good explanation for his parking his lorry so that people could only squeeze into the hotel one at a time.

On the camp itself, one large hangar had been equipped as a cinema and one evening was showing the film of the supposed Jack the Ripper, the part being played by an actor named Laird Cregar, who looked sinister in the extreme. It was a very frightening film and afterwards the WAAFs walked back to their quarters in huddled groups while some of us repeated sentences and noises from the film and very unkindly terrified the WAAFs even more. On another occasion Ted Heath and his band gave a show on the stage. They were the tops in big bands in this country and, while their performance was brilliant, the sheer noise of it was deafening, much like present day and now I would not go near a pop concert.

The unit concerned itself with teaching ex-Spitfire pilots to fly Typhoons and my part in the process, once the pilot could be trusted with a Typhoon, was to teach dive-bombing and ground strafing in small formations. As a job it had its points but the aircraft were old and given to faults, which did not do anything to lessen my nervous tension. After only a few weeks I was despatched to London to attend a selection board for a transfer to Training Command, which needed ex-operational pilots to train as instructors, and this led to my being posted to No. 2 Flying Instructors' School at Montrose in Scotland, which meant a long and wearisome train journey.

It may have been on this journey that I had to change at Crewe late in the day, with no trains for several hours to where I needed to go in order to connect with the LNER east coast line. The Women's Voluntary Service ran a very efficient system. After serving a cup of tea and a sandwich, or something, they would ask what train you wanted to catch. You gave them the time and then they issued a 'bunk number' to you. Tiered bunks had been put into what had been a large waiting room. You climbed into the one carrying the number given. A member of the WVS would come and wake you fifteen minutes before the train was due. With the incessant movement of servicemen up and down the country, the WVS worked wonders and they were a dedicated group of women. They were later to add 'Royal' to their title to become the WRVS.

Chapter 14

Instructors' course at Montrose

And so to Flying Instructors' School at Montrose on the east coast of Scotland, an extremely frigid place in mid-winter. The local schoolchildren seemed to be able to run about without overcoats while we huddled in our great coats and cursed the cold. I started flying there in December 1944.

At Montrose there were, I believe, twenty-four of us on our course, divided into two flights. We lived in wooden huts which had six small single rooms on each side of a central corridor with an ablutions portion at the end. These huts were situated in the grounds of a fine country house which served as our mess, with a bar, refectory and ante-room complete with a grand piano. It was pleasant enough. The bar was rowdy like an operational one and the food was good except for a surfeit of venison, which came about by reason of the group captain going deer stalking and then obliging the mess officer to buy the venison.

One of our number was a Flight Lieutenant DFC with a most unusual story as to how he won his decoration. He had been a 'catapult' fighter pilot. This involved a merchant ship that had a catapult fitted to its fore-deck. The fighter with pilot was fired off in the middle of the ocean to chase off enemy aircraft. Having done so, the pilot had the choice of parachuting into the sea or ditching his aircraft when the navy would pick him up. It never ceased to amaze me that anyone would volunteer for such a perilous operation, but many did so in spite of the very low expectation of survival.

Our course member had been in an Arctic convoy to Murmansk, when he was fired off against a German bomber attack. He shot down the formation leader and while the others broke up in the face of quite unexpected opposition, he shot down another two. No mean feat. After this he found the idea of a dip in the Arctic singularly unattractive. If he was not picked up in two to three minutes he would be dead, due to below zero temperatures. He carried an outline map of Northern Europe and Russia. Knowing his own position with some accuracy, in a strong westerly wind he decided to set course for the nearest Russian territory, hoping his fuel lasted for the necessary distance. It did and he crash-landed just inside Russia where he was found by Red Army soldiers. He was sent by stages to Murmansk and he got there before the convoy arrived. He returned by cruiser. He well deserved his DFC. Strangely, he subsequently died in an accident in a light aircraft.

On the flying side we had a pep talk from a squadron leader to which few paid much attention because none of us liked being in Training Command and really couldn't have cared less what he had to say, until we sat up and listened to his telling us that a certain pub in Montrose was for the exclusive use of instructors and staff and we could drink anywhere but there. *Something had to be done*, as I shall show later.

We were without doubt the toughest and most bloody-minded course ever to be at Montrose. We were all ex-operational, many with decorations to prove it. Once we started flying this attitude became less marked when we all realised we did not know the first thing about flying by the book, with absolute precision, to a set of rules set in stone, no exceptions permitted. Great credit was also due to the instructors, none of whom had ever had squadron experience. Their expertise was such that I could not help aspiring to it, and taking the mickey, as we tried to do, went right over their heads.

Our first morning in our flight dispersal hut started with an instructor coming in, calling one of us by name and barking out AVTB (the four letter sequence identifying a particular aircraft). The pilot (who knew perfectly well what the instructor meant) said, 'What, please, is an AVTB?' The instructor, who knew perfectly well that the pilot knew perfectly well what he meant, did not react but went to the aircraft with his trainee following. So began our introduction to Training Command type of flying. We were given a demonstration of an exercise by an instructor and then were required to perform it ourselves, all the time learning the instruction 'patter' by heart word for word, which was designed to convey to a pupil with the minimum use of words what the exercise was for and how to do it, giving a demonstration then commenting on the pupil's success or otherwise in performing it. The 'patter' was exceedingly tedious but ensured that by following it, only the necessary information was passed and nothing was inadvertently omitted.

Even the basic business of 'circuits and bumps' was quite complex. After completing the cockpit drill (also with 'patter') the pilot requested permission to take off. This being given, the throttles were opened to max power and the aircraft was lifted off at a precise air speed, the precise angle of climb was established then the wheels were retracted, followed by the flaps. The throttles were brought back to make a precise speed and angle of climb and the engine gills were closed. Levelling off at 1,000 feet, throttles adjusted for cruising power while the mixture control was put from 'rich' to 'lean'. A 'rate one' turn was then made to cross from right to left of the airfield, followed by another to establish the 'down-wind' leg of the circuit

No. 59 Flying Instructors' course. No. 2 Flying Instructors' School, Montrose – instructors and pupils

and so on and so on. The approach and landing were similarly subject to a rigid drill.

There were numerous exercises and trainee instructors flew in pairs, one acting as trainee and the other as instructor and at intervals resident instructors took trainees up to check for accurate flying and the everlasting 'patter', while also introducing other exercises. The exercises I learned were of course identical to those I had learned as a pupil at Kidlington nearly four years earlier. The exception was that at Montrose we did no low flying. This may have been due to the local topography. There was a narrow coastal strip which was level but of course the Grampians loomed very close to the north and the Sidlaw Hills to the south. This meant that there was only a corridor down to Perth, which was used by the aircraft from the airfields on the River Tay, which we would meet head on. Some way to the north there was a large airfield which only served as a vehicle park. Apparently, there was such a down-draught from the Grampians at certain times that flying became dangerous. I have no doubt that the local people could have warned the authorities of this had the latter taken the trouble to ask.

At the same time we received ground instruction on airframes and engines and aerodynamics. Most of this was of high quality but the 'engine' man was of the school of an army corporal explaining the firing of a rifle and saying 'yer pulls the trigger and the bullet goes down the barrel with the gases in 'ot pursuit.' He was dealing with ignition systems when he said, 'And what is the condenser (now called a 'capacitor') for?' and we would all yell 'to prevent arcin', sparkin' and burnin'.' Even in a pub in the evening, if someone said, 'What is that for?' no matter what the subject, we would all chant, 'Arcin', sparkin' and burnin'.'

I was very keen to do well and told the squadron leader who had given us the first pep talk that the engine man was not up to the job of giving us real information on engines, in spite of being such a nice person. When the squadron leader put the idea of replacing the engine man to the whole course, it was shouted down and so I kept quiet.

Reverting to the prohibition of trainees going into the 'instructors only' pub, a number of us went into town one night, and after a few pints at another hotel set off for the 'off-limits' one where we burst in, loudly demanding pints of beer and slapping our instructors on the back saying, 'Fancy meeting you here.' After causing maximum disturbance we set off after fifteen minutes or so and never went back, having made our point.

In Scotland at that time the pubs were open from 5 p.m. to 9 p.m., but if you were a 'bona fide traveller', which for some reason meant over nine miles, you were entitled to ask for a meal with drinks after hours. We had an arrangement with the landlord of a pub in Marykirk on the North Esk river which was nine miles away that, provided he was given a bit of notice, we could exercise our 'bona fides' with him. So we would arrive by taxi to have a huge 'fry-up' upstairs with drinks, then leaving our dirty plates on the table we could go down to the bar and continue drinking. There seemed to be a spy system in the village which would warn of the village policeman on patrol, at which point we would take our drinks upstairs again. This was a fine arrangement and very profitable for the pub, but it was eventually ruined by one drunken officer refusing to go back upstairs, so the landlord was in trouble and cancelled the arrangement. There is always somebody who will spoil a cosy deal.

I had only one bad scare on the course. We used a satellite airfield called 'Kinnell' to the south-west of Montrose for much of our flying, and in the late afternoon the last pair of trainees would fly back to Montrose. On one occasion there was an instructor needing to get back and he flew the aircraft with us two trainees sitting behind on the main spar of the wing. After a short while the aircraft began to shake violently, so much so it seemed unlikely to stay in one piece. The instructor turned to us and shouted, 'Should we leave her?' We said nothing. He was in charge and if he had said 'jump' we would have jettisoned the door and parachuted out, but he could not make up his mind and while he dithered he allowed the aircraft to cross the coast and we were headed out into the North Sea, with a strong following wind giving us a ground speed of about 200 mph.

Baling out was no longer an option; landing in a parachute miles out in the freezing waters of winter would be fatal. The instructor's mind was now made up for him and he turned towards land, with the aircraft still shaking violently. We eventually landed safely though badly frightened. The trouble was traced to one of the 'walk-ways' over the wings used by ground crews which had come unstuck at the leading edge and was standing up only a few inches and this had caused the buffeting on part of the tailplane. Such a fright for so little a problem.

On the camp there was a fully equipped gymnasium presided over by a civilian, as far as I can remember. I became reacquainted with the vaulting horse, boxes and ropes that I had last seen at school. Gymnastics was not my particular forte, but nonetheless I enjoyed the experience. We used the gym in bad weather mostly and the 'gym master' tried to be a bit of a martinet. He would not allow any crossed arms in the gym but insisted that we held our arms behind our backs when still. This began to jar a bit. He had us playing a ball game of some sort and he used his whistle every few seconds to ensure the rules were followed. Eventually we got fed up with this and so opened the door and bundled him out, shutting the door on him. After this we had a very violent game and to hell with the rules, while the 'master' took the hint and stayed outside. After thirty minutes or so we called it a day. We were all sweaty and bruised and had left some skin on the floor, but we were relaxed after a good workout, even if there hadn't been any rules.

The CFI at Montrose had his very own aircraft, a white painted 'Albermarle' torpedo bomber. How he was able either to acquire this or keep it I do not know, but he came unstuck after it was sent into the hangar for servicing and an absent-minded or ignorant rigger failed to 'cross' the elevator wires. (This is necessary to cause the elevators to rise when the control column was pulled back and vice versa.) The result was that when the CFI did an air test he allowed the aircraft to lift itself off the ground, then when he eased back on the control column it dived into the mud of the Montrose basin. The CFI was not hurt but had the indignity of having to sit there until the tide came in and someone could row a boat out to collect him some time later. I do not know how the aircraft was removed from the mud.

In the servicing hangar itself there was a large jagged hole in the roof. Upon enquiring as to the cause of this we were told that a mechanic was dismantling an 'oleo' undercarriage leg with a large spanner without taking the elementary precaution of letting the pressure out first. On the last turn of the spanner there was a loud bang and the leg was fired upwards by the high pressure and went, complete with spanner attached, through the roof, hence the jagged hole.

In the main street of the small town of Montrose there was a café we used to frequent when off duty. At intervals of a week or so it received a small barrel full of broken eggs with shells removed, so once we knew which day this was coming, some of us would troop in and have six-egg omelettes with fresh bread and butter and a mug of tea. Food rationing did not seem to function in the Scottish countryside.

One evening we were drinking in the best hotel when it started to snow heavily. Everyone drank up and left to trudge back to camp, but I asked the landlord if he had a room to spare. He said that he did and so I stayed the night. This proved to be a mistake. While the next day was fine and sunny, there was now over two feet of snow through which I had to wade, getting my trousers, socks and shoes soaked through. I do not remember how long it took me to get back, but I regretted having stayed the night.

During that bitter winter of 1944–45 we ran short of wood to light our stoves with and some of us were attempting to chop up some logs, which were piled at the back of the mess. Our attempts were pretty useless and an Italian POW came up and held out his hand for the axe. After some hesitation we gave it to him and he put on a display of skilled wood-chopping while we watched in admiration. After only thirty minutes or so he had chopped enough for all of us. Then he put down the axe and took a few cigarettes from us as his reward.

There were two officers at the station worthy of special mention. The first of these was a squadron leader who had been a professional wrestler and was the strongest man I had ever met. He used to perform for us on occasions, lifting people who stood on his hands or feet from a prone position and so on. He had performed the 'shadow wrestling' part of a film about Henry VIII. Unfortunately for him, he had a short fuse and when he told the driver of a vehicle outside the mess to move it to another position the driver declined, whereupon the squadron leader opened the driver's door and, with one arm, flung him ten feet away. Then he moved the vehicle himself. I do not know what happened to him. The other officer was on our course and he was a classical pianist who played the grand piano in the mess, much to my enjoyment. Funnily enough, out of all the music he played, I remember only one piece and that was not classical at all. It was called 'Gloomy Sunday' and it made me feel gloomy just listening to it.

At Christmas a party started which went on until New Year with breaks for eating and sleeping. I have never been drunk for a week before or since and the only clear memory I have is being found late at night trying to dig a piece of rock out of the path to our quarters because, for some drunken reason, I had decided that this would be easier than taking a couple of steps round it. Not a recollection that I am particularly proud of.

At the end of three months we had a final test with the CFI who had the grace to say to me that I was the only trainee he felt safe with in night flying, even if I did misjudge the wind during a night forced-landing practice. I believe I came top in the written exams and was in the top half-dozen for flying which meant I might be able to take a test-pilot's course later on, which I very much wanted to do.

We were asked individually where we would like to be posted as an instructor and I chose Kidlington, close to Oxford where my wife lived and, much to my surprise, that is where I went. Usually one felt that the RAF asked you where you wanted to go with the express purpose of sending you somewhere else. I started 20(P)AFU towards the end of March 1945. This was situated at Kidlington.

Chapter 15

Instructor at Kidlington

What I thought of my job as a full-time instructor at Kidlington was simple. I hated it. As an RAF unit it was intolerably dull, without even a smattering of *joie-de-vivre*, and the officers' mess in which I had had so much fun in the other places was also dull and very correct. Not being basically service-minded I found this attitude tiresome. On the flying side, the aircraft were far from being smart and perfectly serviced, as had been those at the instructors' school. Many of them were pretty old, and while the senior NCOs struggled to keep them in good flying condition they mostly had recent recruits under them who didn't know a screw from a nut, with the result that a lot of minor faults occurred and this was making me jumpy. It also had the effect of making me listen anxiously for any noise which might be strange and feel for anything amiss with the controls or instruments. I became very tense and dreaded that something really serious would occur. (How right I was.) I actually started flying on 23 March 1945.

Most of the pupils were NCOs and officers who had remustered from other aircrew functions, such as air-gunners, observers and bombers, to train as pilots. As many of these functions were carried out by people who had failed as pilots, some of them were having a second bite of the cherry. I had one pupil in particular, an ex air-gunner, who really was my *bête noir*. He would brace his feet so hard against the rudder-bar when taking off that he couldn't correct any swing which developed. So if we got off the ground within twenty degrees of where we should have been heading it counted as a success for him. Rather than let him frighten me every flight, I should have put him in for a test with the CFI who would undoubtedly have failed him but I did not want to start off by getting a pilot off the course that way.

In my logbook there is a piece of paper stuck in which authorised me to instruct in low flying down to 250 feet, which was not low flying in my book. Fifty feet was low flying and going down to twenty feet on really flat ground. I found an area which is now Silverstone car racing circuit, on which I believe there was a deserted airfield at the time, where I could indulge myself and my pupil in some real low flying. This I greatly enjoyed. My operational experience of low-flying attacks made no difference to the 'down to 250 feet' official limitation.

It has nothing to do with Kidlington, which is about as far from the sea as it is possible to be in Britain, but low flying over the sea can be safely done down to twenty feet, unless conditions are absolutely still and the sea glassy, when it becomes very difficult to judge height. This takes me back to Biggin Hill days when an Aussie pilot, presumably realising he was almost touching the water, pulled the stick back too sharply, with the initial effect of pushing the tail down, and the pilot perished, hitting the sea at more than three hundred mph.

One day when it was pouring with rain I had the men picket the aircraft, clean their shed where they kept their tools, then told them at about 4 p.m. to pack up early. Within minutes of this the phone rang, the CFI demanding to know what the men walking out of my flight dispersal hut were doing. I said there was nothing at all for them to do so I gave them a break. 'Gave them a break?' he said, his voice going up a couple of octaves. 'Report to me at 09.00 hours tomorrow.'

Now I realised that I had not thought about every airman/woman on the airfield expecting the same treatment when it rained, but when the CFI was giving me a real bollocking next morning I thought what a miserable creature he was. He simply couldn't get his head round the idea of 'giving the men a break'. He was, I believe, a 'regular' officer, which may have explained it.

At some stage the officers' mess threw a party to include wives and girlfriends (and no doubt some others). This was the only fun occasion and my wife was invited to open the buffet with the station commander, which pleased her a lot. She managed to put a few very tasty sandwiches in her handbag for her Mum.

Returning to the flying, my friend, the ex air-gunner, was my pupil again when we took off in a thick haze below cloud and there was not a breath of wind. We were on a navigation exercise and after about twenty minutes we had a total systems failure. The warning lights flickered and went out, while the radio and intercom went dead. The hydraulic and air pressure dropped to zero, which meant there was no means of getting the undercarriage down, no flaps and no brakes. Somehow I had to get the aircraft on the ground without killing the pair of us. Not being willing to fly a crippled aircraft back across country in a thick haze, I turned east and picked up the Oxford – Banbury railway line and turned south to follow it.

A half-turn to the right after we passed the grain silos brought us to Kidlington, where I flew past the watch office waggling my wings, having no other means of communication. I selected 'undercarriage down' then climbed to the cloud base and did a few short dives with very sharp pull-outs to try to shake the wheels down. I flew past the watch office again and, as they did not fire a red light, it obviously looked as if the wheels were down, but that did not mean they were locked down.

I flew round and coming in very low I bounced my wheels on the ground while I still had flying speed. They held, so I shut off the engines and the fuel and steered the aircraft on the rudder to a far corner, which would give an extra 100 yards or so to stop in. We bounced over the perimeter track on the far side then ran into very rough ground, which slowed us up, and we finally stopped about ten yards short of a stand of big trees.

I would have done the landing in a less risky way had I thought of it. After bouncing the wheels on the ground, I should have gone round again, made an approach just above stalling speed and then dropped it to the ground. This would probably have reduced the landing speed by ten or fifteen mph. My pupil, who apparently had a blind faith in my ability to avoid killing us, helped me out of the aircraft, where I collapsed and was taken to the sickbay where the doctor said, 'You are grounded.' Thus ended what I had hoped would be a career in flying. It was 13 May 1945. It was subsequently found that the auxiliary drives at the back of each engine, which supply compressed air, hydraulic pressure and electricity for the aircraft services, had been incorrectly installed after servicing so that the drive shafts had sheared, hence the shutdown in systems.

VE Day came in June and we celebrated by everybody congregating on the airfield where every signal rocket, Very light and signal mortar were fired off. It made a fine show and much drink was taken.

The only additional thing I remember was a flight sergeant who decided that the best way to clean the greasy floor of a hangar was to pump a large quantity of petrol onto it and then get the men to brush it over. He took an appalling risk and the slightest spark from somewhere would have blown up the hangar and half the camp with it. I don't know whether this ever reached the engineering officer's notice or perhaps the flight sergeant got away with it.

After finishing flying I got permission to live out of the camp and my wife and I took up residence in her sister's house with her husband. I rode the ten miles odd by bicycle to camp each day and was badly frightened one day when a young cow suddenly burst through a hedge and came galloping towards me in the middle of the road. I was paralysed with fright but let out a loud shout, which caused the animal (which was probably as frightened as I was) to veer round me and gallop off down the road. No one came after it and what became of it I never knew. I recovered myself and went on to camp.

Once I had finished flying I had to take my share of being orderly officer of the day. One of the duties was to visit any satellite units which held code books of any sort to check that they were being held securely. The only satellite station was the night-flying neon beacon, a large piece of equipment that had to be towed to a different location every day, often down country lanes and across muddy fields. The transport provided for me was a motorbike and sidecar. I stepped into the uncomfortable thing and the rider snapped on the hood making me a prisoner. He then kick-started the motor, which immediately burst into flames. I thought 'My God, have I survived all this time only to be burnt to death in a bloody sidecar.' The rider, however, was used to this performance. He stuffed a rag up the air intake and doused the flames. To say that I was relieved would be an understatement of the highest order.

In June my wife's father died and so we moved into her mother's house to keep her company in her great distress. It was about this time that my wife gave me £100 (I never had a bean of my own) and I bought a car from a fellow officer on the camp. It was a 1934 Riley 12/6 with triple carburettors and a commensurate thirst. It ran on only 5 psi oil pressure when hot instead of a more normal 50 psi, indicating much wear within. The back seat was pneumatic and had to be blown up by mouth. It had pre-selector gears and the control handle broke off, making changing gear somewhat difficult, until an airman on the camp made a piece of metal to be bolted across the break. By this time I had become the 'Station Signals Officer' and one of my staff was a skilled radio mechanic. We started up a business where I would collect broken radios from people, which I ferried to Kidlington in the car, where we would both service them and then take them back to their owners and charge a fee. This became what is called 'a nice little earner' and the camp authorities never found out.

The telephone exchange in the signals section was manned twenty-four hours a day. A daily roster ensured three eight-hour spells spread amongst the staff, including the airwomen. One night a senior NCO went in for some reason and found the duty airwoman copulating enthusiastically with her RAF boyfriend on the rest bed provided for the night duty staff. He sent the young man packing and reported the airwoman's conduct to me. I thought privately that it was very hard luck to be disturbed in the middle of it, but having had it reported some action was called for. I sent for the girl and not too severely said I could not permit such conduct in the building, which was my responsibility, and if she did it again she would be punished if ever I got to hear about it. She said, 'Yes, Sir' and left. My duty done I moved on to other things.

Under the signals section floor there was a conduit for thick electrical cables, which was covered with a wooden plank. The cables had been removed and when I came in one morning the female staff were in hysterics because they could hear rats under the boards. The camp had a civilian rat catcher with a terrier and we summoned him to deal with the problem. He stationed himself and the terrier at the conduit exit and said, 'You puts an 'ot poker in the other end, sir,' which we did. The rats streamed out and the terrier dealt with them all, although it got badly bitten in the process. The exit was sealed and the problem was solved.

Before being posted to Penrhos in North Wales, I sold the old Riley to a dealer who saw fit to pay £100 for it, so my wife got her money back. I had hoped that I would use some of the money to pay my mess bill, but my wife said that it had taken her ages to save the £100 (about £5,000 today) and so I would have to pay my own mess bill. She was quite right, of course.

Chapter 16

Remaining Service Period

As the station at Kidlington continued to run down, I was posted to Penrhos near Pwllheli, on the southern side of the Lleyn Peninsula, along with about a hundred other redundant aircrew. I cannot put a date to this move, but I remember beautiful weather at the end of October 1945 so the move presumably took place a little earlier than that. Being put out in the wilds without anything to do at all brought on the most frightful effects of my shattered nerves. This caused such mental anguish at the time and these effects lasted over a period of three years or more before some nervous stability reasserted itself with the help of a very old-fashioned GP whose practice we came under as a family after my leaving the RAF.

At Penrhos not very much happened, but one occasion comes to mind shortly after my arrival. The weather was brilliant and a colleague and I decided to walk across the Lleyn Peninsula to a hill on the north side, which was clearly visible, and perhaps climb it. We started off going direct across country through farms, the occupants of which took a dim view, although what damage we could possibly do was a mystery. We also encountered numerous wild sheepdogs, which came for us barking loudly, and we were scared by this (not knowing that sheepdogs are trained not to bite). We finally arrived at the foot of the hill but were too exhausted to attempt to climb it. We went back walking on the road, which was safer but much further. By the time we got back we just made dinner then went to bed.

The Station Commander, a group captain, used a Magister training aircraft as his personal transport and one day he rang up to be fetched by car in a field in which he force-landed. The engine failure apparently resulted from the petrol tank having some water in it, though whether it was put in on purpose or accidentally was a mystery. His one other claim to fame was when he decided (probably when drunk) to drive the station's flock of geese through the officers' mess. The term 'shit-scared' is well known and this certainly affected the geese. One could not imagine that a dozen birds could make such a mess and the group captain was pleased with his effort to lighten the tedium of being in such a place. The unfortunate mess staff had to clean it up and there were some audible complaints about it, not such a surprise.

There is nothing much more to be said about Penrhos, except that the group captain sent for me one day to tell me that he had been asked to recommend whether I should be put on the 'lack of moral fibre' list which, if confirmed, would lead to a parade at which one's jacket buttons, wings and decorations were stripped off and one was discharged with ignominy. This was because I rashly said at some stage that I did not wish to resume flying. This, after two tours of operations and a DFC, was beyond belief. The group captain asked me to let him have my flying logbook, in which fortunately I had made notes against all my operational flights, giving brief details of the fighting and ground attack operations. After a short period I got my logbook back and was told to forget it. I was greatly relieved.

At some time in the early part of 1946 I was sent with others to selection boards for our future use. These boards were situated at Eastchurch on the Isle of Sheppey (the oldest airfield in the UK) and it seemed typical of the RAF to place a lot of officers in North Wales and then send them for reselection at an even more inaccessible place on the Kent coast. Journey time overall was twenty-three hours. I put most of my baggage in the Force's luggage room at Paddington and took a small case to stay overnight at Eastchurch.

In appearance Eastchurch airfield still looked like pictures of the First World War. Even the huts looked as if they had been there since 1914 and probably they were. A number of officers shared the huts and the next morning attended individual selection boards, where I was informed that my posting would be to the New Zealand aircrew repatriation unit as adjutant, then situated at the Metropole Hotel in Brighton. The nearby Grand Hotel was occupied by Australian aircrew, or it may have been the other way round.

There was an incident when I went to Paddington to reclaim my baggage. I was third or fourth in the queue, which was led by a very angry, probably drunken Canadian soldier who had unwisely put his own baggage and that of his friend on the one ticket, but only wanted his own out. The counter hand said, 'You takes the lot or nothing' at which the soldier produced a large revolver, waved it at the unfortunate man behind the counter and said 'Gimme my f——ing baggage, you bastard.' The cockney behind the counter vanished like a rabbit down a burrow and scuttled off to the rear. The Canadian roared, 'I'll get the bastard' and ran outside waving his gun, presumably intending to go in at the back to sort them out. He ran straight into a very large military policeman who disarmed him and slammed him to the ground, where he was still holding him when I came out. The 'gentle touch' was not in an MP's vocabulary.

I reported to the hotel in Brighton where I met the CO, a Wing Commander Colville, who made up for his dreadful injuries by having a very forceful personality. At sometime during his service he had made a forced landing in which his feet were broken off backwards. The surgeons put them back but could not repair the joints so the wing commander's feet were attached rigidly to his legs and he could walk only in a sort of waddle. He made light of this and his men worshipped him. After introductions had been made, he took me to a room, which was to be my office and said, 'Smithy, this is where you work and on no account are you to venture upstairs. That is my job.' There was a lot of violence amongst the aircrew, largely due to gambling, and the central stairwell was wired with heavy gauge netting to prevent people being thrown down to the ground floor. I can't remember but there must have been a lift for the CO to use because he used to go up late at night and scatter the gambling games with his stick and none of the men touched him.

Orders were received to move the unit lock, stock and barrel to a camp at a place called Moreton Valence in Gloucestershire, which none of us had ever heard of. Our parent station for rations and pay was to be Little Rissington also in Gloucestershire, at that time the Central Flying School. The distance between the two was, I believe, about forty miles and beyond Gloucester itself. It was a very hilly run.

The CO rang up someone to enquire who had been at the camp and the answer was Italian POWs. He then asked if all the Italians had left and the answer was that there were a few still there. The CO refused to move the unit until he was assured that all the Italians had left because he had a few Maoris amongst his men who would slit the Italian throats without a second thought. I have forgotten why the Maoris so hated the Italians. Eventually I was able to raise a 'movement order' to transfer the unit to Gloucestershire. We were to go by train, of which I had the doubtful pleasure of being in charge. After what seemed a long journey we arrived at Gloucester station where I tried to get all the aircrew onto service buses to go to Moreton Valence. Quite a lot of them took no notice and wandered off into the town to see what it had to offer in the way of girls and beer, but by the next day there were all back in camp, much to my relief.

At the start we had a large unit complete with a medical officer, sick quarters and a compliment of service women (always called WAAFs) with two female officers (of which more anon). They were quartered in huts equipped for female personnel about 200 yards down the road where they could not effectively be guarded, but it was a bit out in the wilds with very few young men about and so the risk to them was not great. The HQ of the unit was a wooden hut by the airfield, which contained the wing commander, myself and an orderly room, where some of the girls may have worked as clerks. I was always amused by the contradiction in terms between the 'orderly room', which was an untidy area of 'in', 'out' and 'pending' trays, all full of bits of paper, and the 'mess', with its immaculately straight lengths of table, and as clean as a new pin except at meal times.

The rest of the female staff worked in the kitchen. There were airmen's, sergeants' and officers' messes running and it takes a lot of staff to operate all three at once. The female officers had disciplinary control and had to handle complaints and settle arguments, as well as allocating the women to their various duties.

Among the New Zealand officers and NCOs the biggest one by far was nicknamed 'Tiny'. He was about 6′6″ and weighed 15 stone but fortunately he was mild mannered. His only fault was that soap and water and Tiny did not mix. He was not known to bathe or change his socks and his battledress looked as though it belonged to a tramp. At the other end of the scale we had a Maori who was shy and self-effacing but like so many of his race was physically very powerful. I commented to Tiny and some of his colleagues on this and was told that I should run for my life if he ever drank any alcohol. I will call him Jimmy. One evening I was sitting in the mess when Tiny came in and said, 'Jimmy is drunk. Go to your hut, Smithy, and stay there.' I would not normally have accepted being spoken to in that manner even by Tiny but he was obviously very nervous, frightened even, because as the biggest man in camp he would have to take the lead in subjugating Jimmy, who was a great deal stronger and fighting mad to boot. I believe it took Tiny and five or six other tough New Zealand men to batter Jimmy into submission. Next day Jimmy was his old shy self again, although black and blue all over, and all those involved also showed how violent the fight had been.

To return to the female officers, the senior one (always referred to as the Queen Bee) was a very county lady and as tough as they come. The junior was a mouse by comparison, and they each had a single room at the end of the WAAF quarters. On one occasion the Queen Bee was away, leaving the mouse to cope and in the middle of the night she heard a lot of screaming from the women so she went in and found a man there. The mouse sailed into him, throwing punches left and right, and soon had the man pleading for mercy on the floor. The police were phoned and took the man away.

Now our friend Tiny was greatly impressed with the mouse's performance and asked her to go out with him. She must have said if he took a bath, had a shave, changed his socks and wore a decent battledress she would think about it. We were stunned at breakfast next day when a well-scrubbed and smart Tiny came in and he got a terrible ribbing for being a changed man all for a mouse. He took it all in good part, the mouse went out with him and in no time at all they were inseparable. They were married and shipped to New Zealand as a couple. I often wonder how she coped with being the wife of a sheep farmer.

Early one morning I went down to the sick quarters for something or other and found the MO busy sewing back into place a large flap of skin hanging down from under a New Zealand NCO's chin, presumably having cleaned the raw flesh and the skin first. It must have been agonising but the NCO didn't even flinch and while the MO was skilful he was not very gentle, because the horrible injury was the result of the NCO being in bed with a lady when her husband, who should have been on night-shift, came home and wasted no time in hitting the NCO with a broken bottle. He had walked back from Gloucester in that condition and then sat up until the MO was available. I always envied people of great physical hardihood, not being very well supplied with it myself.

As the New Zealand aircrew went home in batches the camp started to run down. Many airmen were posted away and in return we received a batch of new recruits, most hailing from the north-east, which had been an area of great deprivation before the war. Some of these lads were stunted in body after being half-starved all their lives and their accent was almost unintelligible. A few of the recruits, however, were ex-public schoolboys and so there was a real mixture.

The Admin Officer at HQ rang up to say he was having our WAAF contingent posted away, so I asked when their male replacements would arrive. He said airily that they were on their way, but I said that when they had reported for duty the WAAFs could go but not before. I did not usually argue with senior officers but on this occasion it is just as well I did, because the male mess staff did not arrive for another two days.

The unit was now reduced to myself as the only officer, four or five NCOs and a couple of dozen men. I moved into the CO's quarters where I had a nice living room, bedroom and bathroom but we all messed together, myself at a table with the NCOs while the airmen sat at tables alongside. All but one of the NCOs were ex aircrew. The odd one out was a flight sergeant of twenty years service. He was foul-mouthed and chased his men about using a hectoring tone. He was always cheerful and respectful to me and had some amusing stories to tell. I remember a favourite phrase of his when describing someone who had been surprised by something, which was 'his eyes stood out like chapel-f——in'-'at-pegs', this all being rolled into one word. He was of great assistance to me and I made no attempt to moderate his manner towards his men. He would not have understood what I was about. In any case I depended on him to organise the day's work and allocate various jobs which had to be done between the other NCOs and airmen. So he was of great value to me.

I ran camp on a loose rein. My only requirements were:

1. that everybody turned up for work on time, including me.
2. that anyone going out of the camp after work looked clean and smart.

To this end either the flight sergeant or myself stood on the camp gates and sent back to barracks anyone who looked unshaven or untidy. The men soon got the message and, whatever they did once outside, at least they looked like RAF men.

One day I received a letter addressed to the Commanding Officer of RAF Moreton Valence and this was from a solicitor who was acting on behalf of the flight sergeant's wife, asking me to intercede to get him to send more money to her. It was really none of my business but I did tell him that I had received the letter. He grew very angry and said, 'It doesn't matter how much money I send to that bloody woman, she always wants more.'

I said, 'Well, it isn't my business, Chief, and I'll write back and say I have mentioned it to you and that is as far as I am prepared to go.' This I did.

The flight sergeant should have occupied the room at the end of the hut where the men slept, but he asked me if I could give him a room elsewhere in the camp, otherwise he would be found ' 'anging up by his bleedin' thumbs'. I said he could pick his own room as there were plenty to spare in the camp and this he did.

One of my duties was to keep an 'Imprest' account. This gave the unit a certain amount of money for incidental expenses, such as paying the local garage for petrol and purchases of items locally for which it would not be worth sending, especially from Little Rissington. This meant some very elementary double-entry bookkeeping which, nonetheless, caused me a lot of trouble trying to keep it sorted out.

The food was awful and I thought the catering officer at HQ was sending us all the poor rations, as a tiny unit forty miles away, to get rid of them. Having nothing to do one day I drove the ration truck to Little Rissington myself and, leaving it outside the rations store, went across for a pint in the officers' mess, where I met the Wing Commander Flying from Montrose. We shook hands and he said, 'Flight Lieutenant Smith, the aerodynamics man.' I must have made quite an impression at Montrose for him to remember it eighteen months later. Going back to the loaded ration truck I looked into it and was staggered by the beautiful joints of beef and mutton, (whatever happened to mutton?) offal, bacon, cheese and eggs, while sacks bulged with fresh veg and potatoes and there were smaller bags of fruit. This could not be what we had been eating or was our cook a real dud? I decided to act on the latter assumption and arranged an immediate posting for the cook. I then asked for a volunteer to do the cooking and a young ex-miner from Durham said, 'I'll have a go, Sir.' I have no idea whether he had any previous experience but he fed us well.

Our job at Moreton Valence became 'care and maintenance'. We gathered in beds and bedding, lockers, shelving and even three large boxes packed with sanitary towels. All this was stacked in a hangar down on the airfield as the truck went round to collect it and after the day's work the truck itself was driven into the hangar while one of the NCOs locked up. What I did not know until a little later was that the new recruits were terrorised by a couple of senior airmen into leaving the bolts on the hangar doors at the other end in the 'up' position. So after dark these doors were rolled open, the truck was loaded with goods and did a round of pubs a few miles away, flogging blankets and sheets for hard cash. We had not been required to count what we put in there, so a few dozen sheets and blankets could be taken without visibly reducing the stock and more were piling in. This all came to light when the truck driver, a nasty piece of work, reported that his petrol tank had been 'milked' while his truck was parked somewhere, but I did not believe him. I spoke on the phone to the Admin Officer at HQ and he sent in a 'Special Branch' ferret, who discovered the truth in short order and I think six of the airmen were court-martialled and jailed.

I have already described the process by which I arrived as Adjutant at Moreton Valence in Gloucestershire. Amongst the officers we raised a weekly 'news-sheet' which was duplicated several times and was available to anyone who wanted to read it. As the New Zealanders headed for home it was discontinued but kept us amused while it lasted.

The nearest proper officers' mess was at RAF Innsworth two or three miles away on the Gloucester road and I got permission to use it. The main attraction at this unit was 'Bingo' evening, which I attended now and then for something to do, and this usually ended up with drinks in the mess bar. There were German prisoners of war working on the camp and a tough lot they looked, but they were apparently well behaved. After a heavier drinking session than usual, I started to weave my way from Innsworth back to camp and my feet felt very hot and uncomfortable. So I took off my shoes and walked in my socks. Next morning my feet were very sore and my socks were in tatters. Another memory that I am not very proud of.

One evening I realised that an aircraft was circling the airfield, evidently lost or in trouble. I drove quickly to the old watch-office and tried to turn on the flare-path, but the power had been disconnected. Going back to the camp, I phoned Little Rissington to tell them what was happening because I thought that they might be able to contact the aircraft. The helpful message given to me was to signal the aircraft that the airfield was closed. I said, 'How am I to do this?' The answer came 'with an Aldis lamp, of course.'

'But I haven't got an Aldis lamp here,' I replied. The bomber went away in the end.

The part of the camp by the airfield dropped out of use except for the hangar used for storage. There was nothing of any use to anyone except in the old watch-office where there were quantities of leftover electronic bits and pieces, which made a magnet for local thieves. I tried putting men in the watch-office at night but the thieves just said 'Boo' and the men ran away back to safety in their quarters. I asked the local police if they could help us keep the thieves at bay and an Inspector came to look and said, 'There's something wrong 'ere' in a thick local accent, which scarcely seemed an adequate response and nothing was done.

Another incident which comes to mind in which I was involved was one day when I drove the ration truck again to Little Rissington. The truck was a 30 cwt Commer which had no synchromesh gears. Stupidly I slipped the gears into neutral at the top of a long hill going down to Gloucester and the truck raced up to seventy mph and I could not persuade the gears to engage again and the brakes completely faded. The hill flattens out a bit before crossing another main road and, by screaming the engine to full revs, I managed to engage gear again, having shot over the road junction unable to stop. There was not much traffic in those days.

Two other vehicles were in the camp. One of these was a little ambulance with a red cross on the side. I used this as my personal transport, which could have got me into a lot of trouble if anyone at Little Rissington had found out. The other vehicle was a large Leyland lorry which only had a canvas windscreen, did five miles to the gallon and had no brakes. This was used to collect all the stuff from the dispersal sites to put in the hangar, but it was a menace on the road. It also had to be swung by hand to start and usually several airmen had a good swing on the handle one after the other before it sprang into life.

The owner of the local garage from which we bought our petrol came into possession of an old Rolls-Royce of vast proportions. Inside there was a label showing that it had been originally owned by a famous actress of the day. The garage owner asked me if I would like to drive it and, of course, I was delighted to have a go. I would not call it a performance car by modern standards, but it had tremendous pull. It had servo-assisted brakes, driven off a clutch in the gearbox, which could stop the vehicle very quickly. I did have an idea of buying it and taking it back to Oxford to use as a taxi. Fortunately, my lack of ready cash (as usual) meant that the idea was 'no go'. The petrol consumption alone would have bankrupted any attempt to use it as a taxi.

Towards the end of my stay at Moreton Valance, I was instructed to show a small group of civilians, which included a doctor, around some of the empty huts and also the now empty sick quarters, which, under a large layer of dust, was very well equipped. The doctor said he would sell his soul for such a surgery, indicating the sterile taps that he could not get for love or money. This group presumably had hopes of using the camp facilities for civilian purposes.

Another event occurred when I was driving round what had been the WAAF quarters, as part of my job to see that everything was secure and in good order. I saw that one hut was occupied by a civilian family with a bunch of children. They must been making use of service equipment of beds and mattresses and blankets, which didn't much interest me, but I did not know what they might have filched. So I asked our bright young policeman to question them. That was not his style and he just barged in and had a look. I can't remember what he found. I reported this to Little Rissington and the Admin Officer there said, 'Get them out.' I replied that I had no means of doing so and in any case the RAF had no earthly use for all the huts now empty and deserted. This was not popular with the Admin Officer, but there was nothing he could do about it.

On the other side of the airfield the Gloucester Aircraft Company had a unit but I cannot remember whether they did any flying. I did meet their chief test pilot Eric Greenwood, who had survived enough forced landings to create a bit of a record. In the course of twelve test flights he force-landed ten times, but by then he got his kicks by tearing down the runway in an old ERA racing car he got from somewhere. He must have had no nerves at all.

My posting for demobilization came and before departing I was required to go to say my farewells at Little Rissington where the group captain was kind enough to say I had done a good job. Back to Moreton Valence where the flight sergeant said the lads would like to have a farewell drink with me, so we all piled into a truck and drove to a pub on the Gloucester Canal where everybody got drunk and presented me with a pint tankard inscribed 'To Flight Lieutenant R.G. Smith, D.F.C. with best wishes from all at Moreton Valence. So my very last job in the RAF, minor though it was, enabled me to leave on a high note.

With many other officers I was posted to Kirkby near Blackpool. Although none of us knew one another, we all went into Blackpool to have a final fling, only to find ourselves abused and threatened by many hundreds of airmen doing the same thing. We left and went back to Kirkby before we got hurt and I don't think any of us had thought that the ranks hated officers so much. (In India there was a full-scale mutiny by RAF men who had been left to stew in their sweltering barracks while the officers went off to the local flesh pots.) The next day we all went to the demob centre where we picked up civilian clothes, were signed off and given a travel warrant home. After the experience of the previous evening we could not wait to get into 'civvies' and become anonymous.

Looking back across more than sixty years I feel a sense of wonderment at the colossal effort put into fighting the war by both the allies and their enemies. The savagery of it all put Genghis Khan and his Mongols in the

The author and his wife dressed up to attend a Masonic Ladies Night by invitation from their oldest friends

shade and the scale of events and loss of life defied belief. The abiding sorrow of all this was the appalling casualty rate suffered by Bomber Command. No fewer than 55,000 young airmen died, which is a higher rate than soldiers in the trenches of the First World War taking into account the numbers involved. I cannot help but feel that different tactics might have achieved 90 per cent of the result with perhaps only 50 per cent of the casualties. I played my small part in this as a fighter pilot frequently in terror, sheer boredom or wild exhilaration. Not a mixture to be recommended for someone of a nervous temperament.

To conclude. For a while – just a few years when it really mattered – a timid youth became a man among men. He was not found wanting. He is very proud of it and, for all the anguish caused by shattered nerves, he wouldn't have missed it for all the world.

Appendix

Notes of general interest not directly connected with the main story

In RAF fighters with Rolls-Royce Merlin engines, full throttle gave, I believe, about eighteen pounds of boost at ground level with 3,000 rpm. This gave a quick take-off. If the throttle was moved a little to the left it could be pushed further forward and this gave twenty-five pounds of emergency boost. This was known as 'going through the gate'. A piece of copper wire was fastened across the gate and if this was broken the engine fitter knew at once that the emergency boost had been used without the pilot having to tell him. This usually led to the engine being removed and sent away for a strip-down overhaul, while a spare engine was fitted. I cannot imagine there was time during the Battle of Britain for this performance. In Malta we went through the gate as a matter of course and no copper wire was there to record the fact. While there were engine failures at times, mostly the serviceability was very good, in spite of the harsh treatment.

The supercharger that provided the boost in the Merlin could probably deliver over fifty pounds at ground level which would have blown up the engine and so a great deal of power was wasted on spinning the supercharger at an unnecessary speed. As the aircraft climbed, the power wasted diminished until the optimum height was reached where the supercharger could just deliver the full boost and no power was wasted. Above this height the power fell off but the aircraft could still function up to about 30,000 feet, at which height the engine ran out of 'puff'.

The Americans used exhaust-driven turbines for supercharging (except the P51 Mustang that had a US copy of the Merlin engine). These turbines were inefficient at low level but got better as the height increased and above 20,000 feet really performed well.

All aircraft were fitted with a propeller 'pitch' lever, with which rpm could be set irrespective of throttle opening. It was controlled by a Constant Speed Unit (CSU for short) operated by engine oil pressure that turned the propeller blades to maintain selected rpm, perhaps for fuel economy. It had limitations in that high boost at low rpm was damaging to the engine. So if maximum power was used the pitch lever had to be moved to give more rpm.

The engine of the German Me109 had the same configuration as the Merlin (i.e. V12) but the engine was installed the other way up. A heavy cannon was installed in between the two cylinder blocks which fired through the propeller boss. While it did not carry much ammunition, if a German scored a hit with it, it was curtains for the RAF fighter on the receiving end. After using the cannon ammunition, the wing-fitted machine guns of the Me109 were used so that the aircraft could keep fighting.

The guns fitted to the RAF fighters were lined up to focus at 250 yards ahead and the gun sight was also focused at the same spot. This gave an intensity of fire that could tear an enemy aircraft apart if dead on target at the correct distance. Later in the war a different gun spread was used to increase the chances of hitting the target, although not with the intensity of the focus.

When running a Merlin engine up to full power against the wheel chocks, it was necessary to have a person on each side sitting on the tail-plane to stop the aircraft rising in the slip stream. This must have been very uncomfortable for these people, to say the least. Some ground staff preferred to face forward, gripping the leading edge tightly, while others faced the rear, doubling themselves over the tail-plane. On one occasion a pilot took off with the airman still over the tail, but managed to get him down again intact. Female ground crew had to do this as well and I remember when one had just got off the tail after being bent over it and an airman standing by rudely said, 'That will cool it down a bit.' The girl blushed and held her tongue.

By 1944–45, fighter aircraft such as the Tempest (a development from the Typhoon but with a thin elliptical wing) and the Griffon-engined Spitfire (the airframe had to be extensively altered to deal with the power of this 37-litre engine) were reaching speeds of over 470 mph at low level, which is about as fast as a propeller-driven aircraft can be persuaded to go.

It astonishes me that in 1934 a monoplane mounted with two enormous floats and external wire bracing reached 430 mph in the Schneider trophy race using a two-bladed fixed-pitch propeller and without stressed skin/ monocoque construction or anything remotely modern in Second World War terms. I believe the engine was only able to run for thirty minutes or so at full power, as it was very highly supercharged. It was an incredible achievement and one that led to the development of the Rolls-Royce Merlin engine that was so essential for the allies in the Second World War as it powered the Hurricane, Spitfire, Mosquito, Lancaster bomber and P51 Mustang, a record if ever there was one.

Index